Hendrix

the Complete Guide *to his* Music

OMNIBUS PRESS
London/New York
Paris/Sydney/Copenhagen
Berlin/Madrid/Tokyo

Peter Doggett

Contents

INTRODUCTION

JIMI HENDRIX'S 'OFFICIAL' RECORDING CAREER LASTED ALMOST EXACTLY FOUR years. The first two were marked by a Herculean work-rate and awe-inspiring artistic progression. The last two were a morass of indecision, lack of direction, and encroaching depression, accompanied by a dedication to his craft that was even more admirable under the adverse circumstances.

When he died in September 1970, all the talk was about what might have been. In his own mind, though, Jimi had long regarded himself as a failure, unable to build on the creative and commercial success of his first three albums – unable, in fact, even to complete a single studio project since then.

Jimi's untimely demise marked the beginning of a long-term exploitation exercise that has spawned literally scores of albums since 1970. The initial rush to cash in on his death was predictable, but the subsequent saturation of the market demonstrated Hendrix's catch-all appeal to several generations of rock fans, from his original admirers to those who were born years after he choked to death in a London hotel.

There are currently well over 100 'legal' Jimi Hendrix CDs available in shops and on websites, plus twice as many again on the underground bootleg circuit. The purpose of this book is to steer listeners new and old through the chaos that awaits anyone who checks out the Hendrix rack in their local megastore. Faced with the profusion of repackages and rip-offs, even the most hardened rock consumer can be forgiven for needing a friendly guide.

The book is divided into four main sections. After a brief chronology of Jimi's life and career, and a thumbnail sketch of the main protagonists in his story,

Section 1 details the Official Albums – the mere handful of records released in Jimi's lifetime.

Section 2 covers the Posthumous Albums, but only those which have been released by, or with the co-operation of, the executors and trustees of his Estate. These have been divided into two groups: the current (as of 2004) catalogue prepared by Experience Hendrix; and earlier releases, plus those targeted at a limited rather than mainstream audience.

Section 3 surveys the plethora of Unofficial Albums. These cover everything from Hendrix interviews to haphazard collections of his pre-fame work as a session guitarist, via illicitly obtained live tapes and unsupervised rehashes of the official catalogue. The one thing they have in common is that they all are, or have been, on sale in legitimate record stores in Britain and America, and have therefore (often only by a legal loophole) escaped the 'bootleg' tag. Finally, the book ends with Section 4 – a brief listing of Jimi's guest appearances with other artists, plus a guide to their availability on CD.

Even this listing of 'official' CDs scarcely touches the surface of Jimi Hendrix's recording career. Collectors and fans have access to an underground network which supplies them with hundreds of hours of officially unreleased concert tapes, studio out-takes, jam sessions and interviews. An inveterate chronicler of his own musical dabblings, Hendrix kept tapes of his composing stints, rehearsals and after-hours collaborations with fellow musicians.

What turns the obsession of the collector into the search for the Holy Grail is Hendrix's almost superhuman proficiency as a guitarist, and his endless quest for artistic innovation. As a musician, Jimi pioneered a form of expression that encompassed everything the technicians could throw at him, and burst through all known genre barriers. As an artist, he had a vision of a union of experimental music, poetic lyrics and spiritual awareness that has inspired generations of musicians and writers.

Champions of rock, jazz, funk, soul, blues and the avant-garde have all tried to claim Hendrix as their own. He remains the most complete musician ever to have performed rock'n'roll – and the irony is that much of his reputation is based on music which he would never have allowed us to hear if he had lived. His legacy, as documented in this book, proves that four years are quite long enough for a genius to re-make the history of music in his own image.

Peter Doggett
December 1994; May 2004

With special thanks to Stuart Kesting and Stuart Batsford,
without whom...

SECTION 1

THE ORIGINAL ALBUMS

DURING HIS LIFETIME, JIMI HENDRIX APPROVED THE RELEASE OF JUST four albums, one of them a compilation, and tacitly condoned another. Only one was conceived and achieved to his total satisfaction – total, that is, apart from the UK cover artwork, which he deplored.

Are You Experienced and *Axis: Bold As Love* were both completed in 1967, with creative control shared by Hendrix and his manager/producer, Chas Chandler. The two records were assembled with a haste typical of the period: only The Beatles, and to a lesser extent The Rolling Stones, had been allowed *carte blanche* in the studio to work at their own pace.

When Hendrix and Chandler parted company, early in the creation of *Electric Ladyland*, Jimi assumed total command. The album was effectively begun in December 1967, and not completed until August 1968, by which time Jimi had recorded enough raw material to fill several double albums.

And that, remarkably, was the final studio LP of Jimi Hendrix's career. Between August 1968 and his death in September 1970, he completed work on just one single – and that was pulled from the shops within days of release, when he suddenly lost faith in its artistic credentials. Two more LPs were released under his name, but both of them were blatant compromises – *Smash Hits* intended as an obvious stopgap, *Band Of Gypsys* a contractual obligation.

When Jimi died, his next studio record, provisionally entitled *The First Rays Of The New Rising Sun*, was long overdue. Two dozen or more tracks were in various stages of completion, but none of them was actually mixed and mastered. It was left to drummer Mitch Mitchell and engineer Eddie Kramer to assemble *The Cry Of Love*, the first of a long series of outside attempts to read the mind of an artist who had apparently lost confidence in his own judgement.

During the decades that followed, *Are You Experienced*, *Axis: Bold As Love* and *Electric Ladyland* were regarded as sacrosanct by those who appointed themselves as Jimi's artistic executors. There was a minor problem with *Are You Experienced*, which had been issued in different forms in Britain and America, but no-one dared to tamper with Jimi's original vision of his early studio catalogue.

These strict guidelines were maintained until 1993, when Alan Douglas – self-selected as the keeper of the Hendrix flame, and effective controller of Jimi's musical legacy for the best part of 20 years – called a press conference at the opening of his Jimi Hendrix Exhibition at the

Ambassador Gallery in New York City. He used the occasion to announce that the increasingly lucrative Hendrix musical Estate was being moved from US Warner Brothers, who'd been controlling the American release schedule since Jimi's death, to MCA. At the same time, he revealed that he had set in motion plans to update the three 'classic' Hendrix albums – to dress them in clothes more appropriate to the dawn of the 21st century.

"Everything in the present catalogue is a budget release," he explained, "and everything's got skimpy packaging. They're all 25-year-old packages. I want to take high-level, contemporary graphic art, put it on the covers, and use the old jackets on the back. I don't want people to think it's a new record: they should know it's a reissue of the original record, with all these new elements that we're incorporating into it."

Questioned about his rights to tamper with Jimi's work, Douglas responded tartly: "Jimi Hendrix is not here. He's been gone for 23 years. He put it into my hands." Fans were quick to disagree with Douglas's assertions, but within a few weeks the new packages were in the shops – bearing artwork that was undeniably stylish but completely out of keeping with the original designs. Critics slammed Douglas for the typos and inaccuracies on the sets; the curator replied that he'd been forced into delivering the packages too quickly, and that the mistakes would be corrected as soon as the initial supplies were exhausted.

Detractors had to agree, however, that the sound quality of the 1993 CDs was a vast improvement over what had gone before. "The same original master tapes were used," explained engineer Joe Gastwirt, "but our digital ears had matured. We were able to stay much closer to the original sound of the masters."

Though most fans were delighted with the contents, if not the presentation, of Douglas' CDs, that was certainly not the end of the story. By 1996, it was clear that the Hendrix Estate was slipping out of Douglas' hands. The announcement in January 1997 that Experience Hendrix – headed by Jimi's half-sister, Janie Hendrix, with father Al close behind her – had won control of the legacy guaranteed that a new generation of reissues would soon appear. Sure enough, the Douglas CDs were swept aside that April, as Experience Hendrix launched a major campaign to reissue all of Jimi's original albums. According to Hendrix's original engineer, Eddie Kramer, who was a key member of the Experience Hendrix team, the 1997 releases marked the first time that the genuine first-generation master tapes had been used to produce CDs. Joe Gastwirt immediately mounted a defence of the original regime, but the dispute only intrigued industry insiders. For the rest of the world, it was a *fait accompli*: Experience Hendrix now controlled both Jimi's music, and the way in which it would reach the outside world. After initial misgivings, most fans accepted and welcomed the new order. At the time of writing, the 1997

CDs have been on the shelves for seven years, and they are unlikely to be revamped until CDs themselves are swept aside by the next wave of digital sound reproduction.

Are You Experienced

THE THREE ORIGINAL EXPERIENCE ALBUMS WERE PERFECT ENCAPSULATIONS of their eras. While *Axis: Bold As Love* testified to Jimi's increasing musical sophistication and *Electric Ladyland* to his boundless artistic vision, *Are You Experienced* (produced by Chas Chandler) looked both backwards, to his years as an R&B guitarist, and forwards to the sonic discoveries to come. Its wide variety of styles and rhythms meant that it lacked the internal unity of his later work, but it is still – particularly in its current enlarged CD format – a valid introduction to his music.

Are You Experienced

(Version 1)

LP release: Track 613 001 (UK), May 1967
CD release: Polydor 825 416-2 (Germany), April 1985

TRACKS: Foxy Lady/Manic Depression/Red House/Can You See Me?/Love Or Confusion/I Don't Live Today/May This Be Love/Fire/Third Stone From The Sun/Remember/Are You Experienced?

THIS WAS THE ORIGINAL UK TRACK LISTING OF THE ALBUM, AS PREPARED BY Hendrix and Chas Chandler in 1967, then shoved onto CD in the mid-Eighties with the bare minimum of thought. There was no evidence of digital remastering on this package, but plenty of annoying hiss and distortion. Typical of the thoughtless, slap-it-out mentality was the retention of the original 1967 sleeve-notes, with their erroneous assertion that Jimi was born in 1947. One diversion: the version of 'Can You See Me?' on this disc was a mild variation on the original LP cut, that first appeared on the US Reprise version of the *Smash Hits* LP.

Are You Experienced

(Version 2)

LP release: Reprise RS 6261 (USA), August 1967
CD release: Reprise 6261-2 (USA), 1985

TRACKS: Purple Haze/Manic Depression/Hey Joe/Love Or Confusion/May This Be Love/I Don't Live Today/The Wind Cries Mary/Fire/Third Stone From The Sun/Foxy Lady/Are You Experienced?

THE ORIGINAL AMERICAN RELEASE OF *EXPERIENCED* NEATLY OMITTED THE album's two weakest tracks, 'Remember' and 'Can You See Me?', in favour of the A-sides of Jimi's first three singles. But 'Red House' was also sacrificed, with the result that US audiences were denied evidence of Jimi's vital blues roots.

The first pressing of the American CD suffered from the same sonic flaws as its UK equivalent. It was subsequently remastered in mid-1989, and reissued with 'RE-1' etched into the centre of the disc (as were *Axis* and *Electric Ladyland*).

Are You Experienced

(Version 3)

Polydor 847 234-2 (Germany), June 1991

TRACKS: As Version 2

WHEN *ARE YOU EXPERIENCED* WAS FINALLY REMASTERED WITH SOME degree of care for the Sessions boxed set, the involvement of Alan Douglas' US team of engineers entailed that it was the American issue of the album that was corrected – therefore becoming the standard, albeit briefly, for the entire world.

Are You Experienced

(Version 4)

Polydor 521 036-2 (Europe), October 1993

TRACKS: Hey Joe/Stone Free/Purple Haze/51st Anniversary/The Wind Cries Mary/Highway Chile/Foxy Lady/Manic Depression/Red House/Can You See Me?/Love Or Confusion/I Don't Live Today/May This Be Love/Fire/Third Stone From The Sun/Remember/Are You Experienced?

AT LAST, A NEW STANDARD FOR A NEW AGE: AN ENTIRELY REMASTERED AND repackaged album, with generic artwork utilising period photos by Gered Mankowitz, brilliantly transformed by the Wherefore Art? design team. The pathetic four page inserts of previous CDs were replaced by a deluxe 24-page affair, stuffed full of informative, if sometimes pretentious, notes by Michael Fairchild. (The reverse of the CD package helpfully explained that the album "is a key to the union of ancient and futuristic urges".) On the back cover of the booklet, alongside a sheet of detachable Experience adhesive stamps, was a reproduction of the original front cover artwork, for the purists among us. (The same approach was utilised for revamps of the *Axis: Bold As Love* and *Electric Ladyland* CDs.)

The track listing was also reworked, with the intention of combining the UK and US contents, plus relevant bonus cuts. To preserve the chronological sequence, the A- and B-sides of the Experience's first three singles were added to the start of the album, before the entire original running order.

There was just one exception to this rule: the version of 'Red House' on this CD was not the one that Hendrix and Chandler approved back in '67, but the fatter, though somehow less exhilarating alternate take, originally released on the American *Smash Hits* LP. Or, as Fairchild put it, "Jimi's vocal is more developed while his guitar lines build flawlessly to a synaptic climax". Nevertheless, its appearance here countermanded Hendrix's original instructions, and was the only serious flaw with this package.

Are You Experienced

(Version 5)

MCA 116 080-2 (US), April 1997

TRACKS: Purple Haze/Manic Depression/Hey Joe/Love Or Confusion/May This Be Love/I Don't Live Today/The Wind Cries Mary/Fire/Third Stone From The Sun/Foxy Lady/Are You Experienced?/Stone Free/51st Anniversary/Highway Chile/Can You See Me?/Remember/Red House

Are You Experienced

(Version 6)

MCA MCD 11608 (UK), April 1997

TRACKS: Foxy Lady/Manic Depression/Red House/Can You See Me?/Love Or Confusion/I Don't Live Today/May This Be Love/Fire/Third Stone From The Sun/Remember/Are You Experienced?/ Hey Joe/Stone Free/Purple Haze/51st Anniversary/The Wind Cries Mary/Highway Chile

IN THE HANDS OF EXPERIENCE HENDRIX, JIMI'S DEBUT ALBUM UNDERWENT another revamp – using, according to remaster engineer Eddie Kramer, the original tape sources for the first time. There were certainly no problems with the sound, which was blistering throughout. Veteran critic Dave Marsh contributed a passionate essay about the album's importance, full lyrics for all the tracks were included and the design of the package was superb.

Sensibly, Experience Hendrix decided to give British and American fans different editions of the album, reflecting the track listing and original cover artwork that they'd grown up with. But the overall contents of the two sets were identical, featuring all the songs issued on the LP (including the correct UK take of 'Red House', at last), plus all the singles and B-sides from the same era.

FOXY LADY

THE ORIGINAL *Are You Experienced* album opened with this feast of sexual innuendo and guitar distortion, set to a slowed version of Wilson Pickett's Memphis soul beat. The first few seconds of vibrato wound up a tension that the rest of the LP rarely let lapse. 'Foxy Lady' was one of the first songs cut for the album, in December 1966.

MANIC DEPRESSION

AN EPIC OF confusion and slightly amused despair, 'Manic Depression' set Jimi's spiralling guitar against the cascading drum fills of Mitch Mitchell. The lyrics caught Jimi between emotional poles, unable to achieve any more coherent response to his world than "It's a frustrating mess". But the guitar solo expressed the point of the song more eloquently, nearly tumbling out of time before Hendrix steered it back into the verse. The track was begun in February 1967 and completed in March.

RED HOUSE

ON MARCH 29, 1967, the Experience taped several versions of this Fifties-style Chicago slow blues. One version, sometimes little more than a tentative jam, but with a sense of discovery that made it irresistible, ended up on the British release of the LP, and, after many adventures, returned to the CD track listing in 1997. The song

was central to Hendrix's vision of his music, remaining in his stage repertoire to the end.

CAN YOU SEE ME?

'CAN YOU See Me?', taped on November 2, 1966, was a contender for the flipside of 'Hey Joe'. Instead, its updated blues theme, built around a nagging guitar riff, ended up on *Are You Experienced*. There was an air of novelty about the entire performance, from its double-tracked vocals to the guitar pulsing from speaker to speaker, but it was undeniably exciting.

LOVE OR CONFUSION

MAGICAL and dark, 'Love Or Confusion' was in a different league to 'Can You See Me?'. Its eerie vocal echo and droning guitar suggested that the second of the two alternatives in the title was closer to the mark. The song dated from the earliest Experience sessions, and was then completed in April 1967.

I DON'T LIVE TODAY

ON FEBRUARY 20, 1967, the Jimi Hendrix Experience stretched rock into new territory with this magnificently malevolent psychic voyage. Even without the grim fatalism of the lyrics, the music alone would have been enough to chart the shift from despair through death into some strange kind of reincarnation, as sirens, dive bombs and animal cries punctuated the tribal ritual of Mitch Mitchell's drums.

MAY THIS BE LOVE

BEHIND almost every song on *Are You Experienced*, Mitch Mitchell unfurled hypnotic, unsettling drum rhythms – even with material as gentle and romantic as this song from early April 1967. Besides the beauty of Hendrix's melody, check the sonic painting of his opening guitar figures, and the spaciness of Chas Chandler's production.

FIRE

INSPIRED by an inconsequential incident at Noel Redding's house on New Year's Eve, 'Fire' returned Hendrix to the R&B circuit, on a song that would have sounded equally at home on an Otis Redding album. Once again, Mitch Mitchell had a field day during the February 3, 1967, session.

THIRD STONE FROM THE SUN

MUSICAL science-fiction became a mini-genre in Hendrix's work with the Experience, pioneered by this instrumental from April 1967. Its riff – later borrowed by Cozy Powell for his 1973 hit, 'Dance With The Devil' – was a throwback to the early Sixties era of surf guitar band; hence the ironic reference during the track's slowed-down dialogue sequence, to the fact that "you need never hear surf music

again". That dialogue proved to be between space commanders, approaching the planet from afar; 'Third Stone' also offered some inter-galactic poetry, and a couple of minutes of tomfoolery on the control-room faders.

REMEMBER

LIKE 'FIRE', this mid-pace song, recorded on February 8, 1967, was proof that Jimi had spent a couple of years on the American R&B circuit. Even the imagery, with its use of soul staples like "mockingbirds", sounded second-hand. Amazing guitar solo, though.

ARE YOU EXPERIENCED?

WIPER-BLADES of backwards tape; drum rhythms from some perverted tattoo; guitars that howled like wounded saxophones; and a voice of blank resignation – these were the constituent parts of a song that begged the answer 'yes', but hinted that the psychedelic journey might not lead the traveller into the light. 'Are You Experienced?' was the strongest track, a four-minute display of all Hendrix's angst and skill in April 1967.

HEY JOE

THE SONG chosen as the A-side of Hendrix's first single had a complex history. It was written by Californian folksinger Billy Roberts, who needed a quick buck and sold it to Dino Valenti, leader of the

Quicksilver Messenger Service. Valenti copyrighted it under the pen-name Chet Powers, and taught the song to his friend, David Crosby. With The Byrds, Crosby began to perform a frantic arrangement of the song in 1965, but before they could record it, they were beaten by fellow LA band The Leaves.

After all that, it was folkie Tim Rose who concocted the slow, bluesy arrangement which, in turn, Hendrix learned in 1966. It became the first song the Experience ever recorded, on October 23 that year, aided by the backing vocals of session singers The Breakaways.

STONE FREE

" JIMI WANTED to put 'Land Of 1000 Dances' on the B-side," recalled Chas Chandler, "but I said no way – you will sit down tonight and write a new song.'" 'Stone Free', a swaggering, hip-speaking piece of rock funk, was the result of this October 24 writing session. Jimi revamped the song in April 1969, as documented on the *Jimi Hendrix Experience* box set.

PURPLE HAZE

FROM ITS ominously out-of-step guitar intro to its howling whammy-bar finale, 'Purple Haze' captured all the threatening adventurism of the early Experience. You could break down the influences, from Stax R&B to the Beatles' *Revolver*, but nothing on earth sounded like 'Purple Haze' in January 1967, when the basic ingredients of this track were cut.

51ST ANNIVERSARY

A CLOSE musical cousin of the album track 'Can You See Me?', '51st Anniversary' was perhaps the most unlikely lyrical concept in the entire Hendrix catalogue – dominated as it was by fantasies of sexual bravado, romance, and excursions into mind and space. '51st Anniversary' tackled the more prosaic subject of marriage and its potential drawbacks – apparently inspired by the collapse of his parents' union many years earlier.

THE WIND CRIES MARY

ON THE same day as 'Purple Haze', the Experience taped this poignant love song, dedicated to Jimi's girlfriend of the time, Kathy Etchingham. Producer Chas Chandler recollected that it took twenty minutes to record, from Jimi's first performance to the band to the final guitar overdub.

HIGHWAY CHILE

C UT AT THE same April 3, 1967 session as the magnificent 'Are You Experienced?', 'Highway Chile' was a relatively lacklustre, if enjoyably unpretentious, piece of rock-blues. It borrowed a guitar figure from the fade of 'Purple Haze', and generally exhibited all the traits of a song composed to order rather than inspiration.

Axis: Bold As Love

ISSUED WITHIN SEVEN MONTHS OF *ARE YOU EXPERIENCED*, *AXIS: BOLD AS LOVE* heralded a new subtlety in Hendrix's work—and a clear mingling of black and white musical inspirations. The début album showed what happened when an R&B musician discovered psychedelic rock; this follow-up made the journey in reverse. Cut almost entirely in the last week of October 1967, with Chas Chandler once again as producer, it was a more unified effort than *Experienced*, but still wavered in mood from electronic experimentation to lyrical balladry, via one overt exercise in political intervention.

Axis: Bold As Love
(Version 1)

LP release: Track 613 003 (UK), December 1967
CD release: Polydor 813 572-2 (Europe), 1987

TRACKS: EXP/Up From The Skies/Spanish Castle Magic/Wait Until Tomorrow/Ain't No Telling/Little Wing/If Six Was Nine/You've Got Me Floating/Castles Made Of Sand/She's So Fine/One Rainy Wish/Little Miss Lover/Bold As Love

LIKE THE REST OF THE INITIAL BATCH OF POLYDOR CDS, THIS RELEASE DID LITTLE to recommend the CD revolution – thanks to some hamfisted editing, dubious mastering, and almost total lack of annotation.

Axis: Bold As Love
(Version 2)

Reissued as Polydor 847-243-2 (Europe), June 1991

TRACKS: As above

SONICALLY IMPROVED, BUT STILL NOT PERFECT (NOTE THE HISS ON 'UP FROM The Skies', as an example), this was the version of the *Axis* CD found in the *Sessions* box set.

Axis: Bold As Love

(Version 3)

Polydor 847-243-2 (Europe), late 1993

TRACKS: As above

THE 1993-STYLE 'OFFICIAL' REMASTERING JOB ON *AXIS* WAS EVERY BIT AS triumphant as the revamped *Are You Experienced*, although this time Alan Douglas didn't add any bonus tracks. Like its companion CDs, this album had its original cover sentenced to the back of the package, while a computer-enhanced Gered Mankowitz photograph fronted the booklet — which had detailed notes by Michael Fairchild.

Axis: Bold As Love

(Version 4)

MCA MCD 11601 (UK), April 1997

TRACKS: As above

THE ORIGINAL COVER ARTWORK WAS RESTORED FOR THE *EXPERIENCE HENDRIX* reissue of the album, which featured an essay by Jym Fahey, full lyrics (although the last four songs were missing from the first run of booklets) and an attractive array of photographs.

EXP

'SYMPHONY Of Experience' was the working title of this tongue-in-cheek representation of the arrival of a creature from outer space – introduced by Mitch Mitchell of "Radio EXP" as "Paul Caruso", who was an American friend of Jimi's. Hendrix's voice supplied the role of Caruso, followed by an exemplary barrage of guitar effects.

UP FROM THE SKIES

AFTER THE sonic assault of 'EXP', the brushed-drums, restrained wah-wah and gentle jazz rhythms of 'Up From The Skies' marked the first of a series of profound switches of mood on *Axis: Bold As Love*. Having unveiled his palette of space noises, our galactic visitor came down to earth, to "the smell of a world that has burned".

SPANISH CASTLE MAGIC

IN HIS late teens, Jimi and his friends used to hang out at the Spanish Castle, a jazz club a few miles out of the Seattle city limits. Almost a decade later, he celebrated its attractions in song – though the lyrical inspiration ("It's all in your mind", he sang at one point) mattered less than the sheer effervescence of Jimi's performance, extended dramatically over the next three years as 'Spanish Castle Magic' became a staple vehicle for jamming during his live sets.

WAIT UNTIL TOMORROW

IF YOU'D crossed 'Stone Free' with 'Fire', this would have been the result – a cool, laidback but still concerned piece of romantic role-playing, wrapped around a sinuous guitar-line, and supported by some white-boy soul vocals from Messrs. Redding and Mitchell.

AIN'T NO TELLING

LIKE 'WAIT Until Tomorrow', 'Ain't No Telling' had its roots in R&B, and Jimi's experiences in roadbands from 1964 to 1966. It was hinged around a call-and-response vocal lick, which ignited into a slyly simple guitar solo.

LITTLE WING

IF MUCH of the Axis album was inspired by Atlantic and Stax R&B, there were also several hints that Jimi had been listening closely to the melodic guitar-playing of The Impressions' frontman, Curtis Mayfield. The lyrical solo which opens the song started with a punctuation mark, and then prepared the listener for the exquisite verbal imagery to follow. Between verses, Mitch Mitchell added some superb drum fills, while the delicacy of the production was perfected by Jimi's one-note-to-the-bar glockenspiel, which supported the emotional fragility of the piece.

IF SIX WAS NINE

IN STARK contrast, 'If Six Was Nine' carried the album's most extreme sound, as the guitar riff and drums combined to create a martial atmosphere. There was no conscious smoothing of the production on this confrontational song, with its free-form guitar solo and equally forceful contribution from Mitchell backing up the radicalism and pride of the lyrics. Recorded in May 1967, five months before most of the LP, 'If Six Was Nine' prefigured the politicised funk of Sly Stone in 1969.

YOU'VE GOT ME FLOATING

BACK TO the bars: 'You've Got Me Floating' was formulaic R&B, in the tradition of 'Ain't No Telling', with only the cross-speaker fades to pull it into the psychedelic age. Backing vocals by Roy Wood, Trevor Bolder, and Ace Kefford of The Move, who were recording next door at Olympic Studios.

CASTLES MADE OF SAND

THE SECOND of Jimi's Mayfield-inspired guitar intros led into a regretful tale of fractured dreams. Some of his most beautiful lyrical imagery explored the failure of a marriage (probably his parents', as on '51st Anniversary'), the realisation of his own artistic limitations, and then in a clever reversal of his theme, the birth of hope from the brink of utter despair. Hendrix never sounded more vulnerable, or more involved in the spirit of a song.

SHE'S SO FINE

ANOTHER abrupt change of mood – and Noel Redding's début as a composer and lead vocalist. His lyrics owed much to the dislocation of British psychedelic pop, from *Revolver* to Pink Floyd, while the music soared from Hendrix-flavoured soul to a blatant tribute to The Who in the middle eight – echoed by Jimi's Townshend-like guitar solo. The high backing vocals were by Jimi and Mitchell.

ONE RAINY WISH

JIMI'S CLOSE study of The Impressions' catalogue inspired another melodic guitar prelude for a suitably misty dream-vision. More than 'Little Wing' or 'Castles Made Of Sand', 'One Rainy Wish' seemed to owe something to chemical stimulation, which would explain the inexact, yet highly colourful, dreamscape Jimi unveiled. Twin guitars cascaded minute variations on a guitar riff, to bring the song to a close.

LITTLE MISS LOVER

FROM DREAM to sexual desire, as Jimi revived the lusty spirit of Don Covay or Wilson Pickett's R&B with a guitar riff that would have delighted James Brown. So would Mitch's drum intro, which cleverly set the pattern for what Jimi played through the rest of the song.

BOLD AS LOVE

THE MYSTERY of the album title was explained in its final song: as Jimi sang, "just ask the axis". That might have been "the axis of the earth", as he claimed in one interview, or some more nebulous spiritual concept; or simply a prettier way of ending each chorus than saying: "You better believe it".

Treading a lyrical tightrope with spectacular skill, Jimi unwound a lengthy personal metaphor with a series of colour images, and then collected the fragments of his soul in the title phrase. After two verses, he decided he could speak more eloquently with his guitar, setting out on a liberating one-minute solo that faded away, then (in what Jimi called elsewhere a 'slight return') regrouped with renewed energy to restate the melodic theme of the song. It was a typically subtle climax to an album divided between R&B dramatics and near-confessional poetry.

Electric Ladyland

FOR PURE EXPERIMENTAL GENIUS, MELODIC FLAIR, CONCEPTUAL VISION AND instrumental brilliance, *Electric Ladyland* remains a prime contender for the status of rock's greatest album. During its 75-minute passage, the album flirted with electronic composition, soft-soul, delta blues, psychedelic rock, modern jazz, and proto-funk, without ever threatening to be confined by any of those labels. It climaxed with a display of musical virtuosity never surpassed by any rock musician. Small wonder that Hendrix found the task of matching this album impossible: despite the splendour of much of his post-1968 work, he could never recapture the effortless magic of *Electric Ladyland*.

The album was a landmark in personal terms as much as artistic. During the early sessions, Chas Chandler effectively resigned as Hendrix's producer; his formal disengagement as co-manager followed the next year. Meanwhile, internal dissension within the Jimi Hendrix Experience ensured that Noel Redding was absent for many of the *Ladyland* sessions. Sometimes Hendrix covered the gap himself; sometimes he augmented his three-man studio line-up to incorporate keyboards, brass or woodwinds.

Most importantly, Jimi was able to expand the visionary painting-in-sound techniques he'd employed on tracks like 'Third Stone From The Sun' and 'EXP', to the point that he was able to build an entire side of the original double-LP – from 'Rainy Day, Dream Away' to 'Moon, Turn The Tides' – into an exotic suite, a seamless composition of fragments and improvisation that couldn't quite be categorised as jazz or as rock. Fracturing those genre boundaries merely made it more difficult for Jimi to reconstitute them in the future.

Electric Ladyland

(Version 1)

LP release: Track 613 008/009 (UK), October 1968
CD release: Polydor 823 359-2 (UK), November 1984

TRACKS
CD1: ...And The Gods Made Love/Have You Ever Been (To Electric Ladyland)?/Crosstown Traffic/Voodoo Chile/Still Raining, Still Dreaming/House Burning Down/All Along The Watchtower/Voodoo Child (Slight Return)

CD2: Little Miss Strange/Long Hot Summer Night/Come On (Part 1)/Gypsy Eyes/The Burning Of The Midnight Lamp/Rainy Day, Dream Away/1983... (A Merman I Should Turn To Be)/Moon, Turn The Tides... Gently Gently Away

THE ORIGINAL CD RELEASE RETAINED THE NAKED 'GLORY' OF THE ORIGINAL album cover, with its parade of slightly distorted female flesh. Hendrix hated that design, and he would have loathed these CDs even more. Not only was the mastering very poor, bathed in hiss and excess noise, but Polydor destroyed the original album concept by combining sides 1 and 4 of the double-LP on the first disc, and 2 and 3 on the second. This magnificent piece of logic meant that 'Rainy Day, Dream Away' appeared after its intended sequel, 'Still Raining, Still Dreaming'.

Electric Ladyland
(Version 2)

Polydor 847 233-2 (Germany), June 1991

TRACKS: ...And The Gods Made Love/Have You Ever Been (To Electric Ladyland)?/Crosstown Traffic/Voodoo Chile/Little Miss Strange/Long Hot Summer Night/Come On (Part 1)/Gypsy Eyes/The Burning Of The Midnight Lamp/Rainy Day, Dream Away/1983 ...(A Merman I Should Turn To Be)/Moon, Turn The Tides... Gently Gently Away/Still Raining, Still Dreaming/House Burning Down/All Along The Watchtower/Voodoo Child (Slight Return)

DURING THE INITIAL PHASE OF REMASTERING FOR THE *SESSIONS* BOX SET, *Electric Ladyland* was sensibly reduced to a single CD (without shedding any of its contents), and the running-order was restored to Hendrix's original instructions. But the sound quality was only marginally more satisfactory than the first release.

Electric Ladyland
(Version 3)

Polydor 847 233-2 (Germany), late 1993

TRACKS: As Version 2

E XCELLENTLY RE-MASTERED, *ELECTRIC LADYLAND* NOW SOUNDED AS breath-taking on CD as it did on vinyl in 1968. Michael Fairchild's notes in the lengthy booklet were superb, and so was the sound quality – from the tumultuous sonic landslide of 'Voodoo Child (Slight Return)' to the delicacy of 'Moon, Turn The Tides' – which, bizarrely, was listed on the back cover as lasting for just one minute, not ten.

Electric Ladyland

(Version 4)

MCA MCD 11160 (UK), April 1997

TRACKS: As Version 2

B RITISH BUYERS SEARCHING THE RACKS IN 1997 FOR HENDRIX'S FINEST ALBUM were doubtless puzzled to be confronted with an anonymously pack-aged set bearing neither the naked artwork that Hendrix hated, nor any-thing more than a small sticker bearing the album title. Instead, this new edition bore the original US cover design, which wasn't what Jimi had want-ed either. Ironically, the Experience Hendrix revision of Electric Ladyland included his handwritten instructions for how the album should be pre-sented – which were ignored at the time, and have been ever since.

That anomaly aside, this package was aimed at a wider audience rather than aficionados, with the late lamented Derek Taylor supplying some typically charming liner notes, rather than the detailed session notes of the previous regime. The sound quality, as elsewhere on the Experience Hendrix repackages, was excellent – though some purists still preferred the results of the 1993 remastering.

...AND THE GODS MADE LOVE

O RIGINALLY conceived under the title 'At Last The Beginning', this solo guitar concoction presaged the multi-dubbed delights to come, as Hendrix conjures magnificence from musical genius and technical brilliance. Taped on June 29, 1968, during a single lengthy session.

HAVE YOU EVER BEEN (TO ELECTRIC LADYLAND)

U NLIKE THE slightly later solo ren-dition captured on the *Jimi Hendrix Experience* box set, this soft-soul classic added studio trick-ery to the obvious influence of Curtis Mayfield's guitar. With Noel absent from the proceedings, Jimi handled the bass as well, and topped off a delightfully airy confection with some precise falsetto vocals.

CROSSTOWN TRAFFIC

HAVING JUST exhibited his command of the most subtle forms of soul music, Hendrix unveiled an aggressive, swaggering funk track – the basic track cut live in the studio by the Experience line-up back in December 1967, and then overdubbed in April and May 1968. Twenty-two years later, the Estate sanctioned the creation of a video to accompany the song's belated release as a single: both visually and aurally, it seemed stunningly contemporary alongside the early 90s funk/rock crossovers of Lenny Kravitz and Living Colour.

Proof that someone at the sessions had a sense of humour was the involvement of Traffic guitarist Dave Mason – whose sole contribution to the track was to sing the name of his band in every chorus.

VOODOO CHILE

THROUGHOUT 1967, Muddy Waters' Chicago R&B song, 'Catfish Blues', became a regular inclusion in the Experience's live set. By early 1968, it had mutated into an original Hendrix song, built around an identical riff, and with lyrics that paid their dues to some of the most unsettling images from the delta blues tradition.

During a lengthy session on May 1, 1968, Hendrix, Mitch

Mitchell, Jack Casady (of Jefferson Airplane) and Steve Winwood (of Traffic) worked their way through a series of lengthy free-form jams around the 'Voodoo Chile' changes. This was the longest, and most successful, with Hendrix's surprisingly orthodox blues playing acting as counterpoint to Winwood's sustained organ chords.

Down the years, there has been much confusion over the exact spelling of this song, and its counterpart at the end of this album. The consensus now is that they should be 'Voodoo Chile' and 'Voodoo Child (Slight Return)'. What matters most, though, is that the two songs – offering vastly different takes on the blues – were the twin pillars of *Electric Ladyland*.

LITTLE MISS STRANGE

FOR THE second album running, Noel Redding was allowed to contribute – and sing – one number. Sadly, 'Little Miss Strange' did little more than repeat the ingredients of 'She's So Fine' from *Axis*, and *Electric Ladyland* would have been a stronger album without it. Like much of this set, it was taped during April and May 1968.

LONG HOT SUMMER NIGHT

HENDRIX doubled up on bass and guitar, while Al Kooper's keyboards took a minor role on this piece of urban soul, which was mixed idiosyncratically, to say the least. Mitch Mitchell's drums were marooned on the far left of the stereo picture, while the other instruments never quite cohered into any kind of whole – as if the tape had picked up musicians in different rooms who happened by chance to be performing the same number.

COME ON (PART 1)

THE FINAL song to be recorded for the album was this cover of a blues by New Orleans guitarist Earl King, cut on August 27, 1968. The Experience ploughed through the standard chord changes and lyrical imagery, for take after take, and several near-identical versions have appeared on bootlegs in recent years. Pleasant but undemanding, its last-minute addition to the album was strange, in view of the fact that Jimi left out-takes from these sessions like 'South Saturn Delta' and 'My Friend' unreleased.

GYPSY EYES

FROM ITS train-in-tunnel drum phasing to its staccato guitar licks, 'Gypsy Eyes' was a masterpiece of creating substance out of little more than a riff and a message of love. Hendrix's guitar patterns on this track, and the interplay he built up with his own bass runs, inspired many later rock/funk crossovers, notably Prince's early-to-mid 80s work.

THE BURNING OF THE MIDNIGHT LAMP

ALREADY issued as a single in September 1967, long before the release of *Electric Ladyland*, 'Midnight Lamp' still fitted the album with its dense production (reminiscent of Phil Spector), unusual voicings (The Sweet Inspirations, with Jimi on harpsichord and mellotron) and evocative imagery. "They said that was the worst record we'd done," Jimi said in 1968, "but to me that was the best one we ever made."

RAINY DAY, DREAM AWAY

ON JUNE 10, 1968, Hendrix, Buddy Miles, organist Michael Finnigan, sax player Freddie Smith and percussionist Larry Faucette jammed through a set of jazzy changes with a cool, late-night feel, and an equally laidback lyric. Suitably overdubbed and edited, their lengthy 'Rainy Day Jam' was divided between this track and 'Still Raining, Still Dreaming'. Initially, it introduced the brilliant suite of music which segued into...

1983... (A MERMAN I SHOULD TURN TO BE)

DELICATE guitar passages established a mood that mixed psychedelic rock and jazz, before Hendrix began to paint in words the portrait of a world torn by war and despair, from which the only escape was the sea. Playing all the instruments apart from flute (supplied by Chris Wood of Traffic, the third member of that band to guest on the album), Jimi created an orchestral tapestry of sound, which flowed elegantly into a gentle chaos of tape effects, backwards guitar, and chiming percussion, and then to...

MOON, TURN THE TIDES... GENTLY, GENTLY AWAY

MULTI-DUBBED guitar motifs restored the psychedelic jazz feel, vamping melodically for several minutes until the mood became almost frenzied, and shifted into an electronically treated drum solo. At last, the familiar themes of '1983' re-emerged, to guide the suite to its conclusion, and complete 20 minutes of stunningly complex and beautiful instrumental tonalities. These two tracks were taped in a single remarkable session, on April 23, 1968.

STILL RAINING, STILL DREAMING

STILL JAMMING, too, first through another verse of 'Rainy Day, Dream Away', and then into a coda which gradually wound down the mellow jazz groove of the original track.

HOUSE BURNING DOWN

ANOTHER collaboration between Jimi and Mitch (Noel Redding played on just five *Electric Ladyland* songs), 'House Burning Down' twisted through several key changes in its tight, swirling intro, and then shifted again as the strident chorus moved into the reportorial verses. Like so many of Jimi's songs from this period, there was an atmosphere of impending doom in the air, inspired by the outburst of black-on-black violence that had shaken many of America's ghettos in recent summers. "Try to learn instead of burn", Jimi advised hopefully, before (as ever) finding salvation somewhere other than the land – this time via a friendly visitor from another galaxy.

ALL ALONG THE WATCHTOWER

'I DREAMED I Saw St. Augustine' was the first song Hendrix thought of covering when he heard Bob Dylan's *John Wesley Harding* at the start of 1968. In 1970, he recorded another song from the set, 'Drifter's Escape'. But it was 'All Along The Watchtower' that made *Electric Ladyland*, and his arrangement was so convincing that Dylan himself has borrowed it ever since.

In its original acoustic form, Dylan threw the emphasis of the song on its apocalyptic imagery. Hendrix used the sound of the studio to evoke the storms and the sense of dread, creating an echoed aural landscape that remains the most successful Dylan cover ever recorded. Dave Mason of Traffic contributed bass and acoustic 12-string guitar to the basic session on 21

January 1968; Jimi completed his overdubs four months later, and the song subsequently became a worldwide hit single.

VOODOO CHILD (SLIGHT RETURN)

TWO DAYS after recording the epic 'Voodoo Chile', Jimi was back at the Record Plant, with Mitch and Noel, ready for this 'Slight Return'. What evolved, over eight takes, was the single most impressive piece of guitar-playing this writer has ever heard, on a track that compresses every ounce of Hendrix's ambition, musical technique, production skill and uncanny sense of impending disaster within five minutes. From its opening wah-wah chatter to the wails of feedback that bring the song to its close, it was an extravaganza of noise and naked emotion. Its verbal imagery was ablaze with destruction and imminent death; and the music was equal to every last nuance. By its very nature, feedback evokes loss of control: during this performance, Hendrix handled it like a wizard controlling a hurricane.

Band Of Gypsys

WHEN CHAS CHANDLER FIRST BEGAN TO MANAGE JIMI HENDRIX, HE QUICKLY discovered that Jimi had left his signature on a bewildering array of record, publishing and management contracts over the previous three years. Chas scampered around New York buying up the contracts, but Jimi neglected to mention the small matter of an exclusive recording deal that he'd signed on 15 October 1965. The contract required that Jimi would, for the next three years, "produce and play and/or sing exclusively for PPX Enterprises", a New York production company headed by one Ed Chalpin (see the Unofficial CDs section for more on PPX, and Jimi's links with the company via singer Curtis Knight).

The PPX deal was hardly lucrative: it entitled Jimi to a 1% royalty *after* all the company's costs had been paid. But it was legally binding, and by signing to Polydor and Warner/Reprise, Jimi had broken it. Writs cascaded in all directions, until in the summer of 1968 Ed Chalpin (now sheltering under Capitol Records' wings) was offered a settlement by Warner/Reprise, which entitled him to the rights to issue Jimi's next album of new material, plus royalties on the first three Experience LPs.

Meanwhile, Warner/Reprise were berating Hendrix for the late delivery of their next album. To ease the pressure, Jimi's manager, Mike Jeffery, suggested that Jimi present Chalpin and Capitol with a live record. To that end, and that end only, Jeffery encouraged Hendrix to assemble a new band as swiftly as possible. And so was born the Band Of Gypsys.

Like The Experience, the new line-up was a trio, teaming Hendrix with his longtime friend, bassist Billy Cox, and the extrovert ex-Electric Flag drummer, Buddy Miles. "We got together to help Jimi out, because he couldn't find anybody else to do it," explained Billy Cox. "With a lot of the music we did, I think Jimi was frustrated because he had a lot of pressure on him. He was being pushed all the time." That frustration began in the studio, where the trio (often augmented by other musicians) made faltering progress towards the Warner/Reprise album. And it carried over to the stage on New Year's Eve 1969 and New Year's Day 1970, when the Band Of Gypsys played their first four live shows at the Fillmore East in New York.

Six songs – four written by Hendrix, two by the over-enthusiastic Miles – were presented to Capitol early in 1970 as the *Band Of Gypsys* album. Ed Chalpin hated it, and so indeed did Hendrix: "I wasn't too satisfied with the album," he admitted shortly after its release. "If it had been up to me, I would have never put it out. Not enough preparation went into it." But Jimi's artistic judgement counted for little against the legal obligation to Capitol, which *Band Of Gypsys* satisfied. The album went Top 10 in Britain and America, regardless of its merits.

Tentative and uncomfortable, the original *Band Of Gypsys* was scarcely a competent record of the Fillmore East gigs, let alone a first-rate Hendrix album. (Both problems were tackled but not really solved in 1999 with the release of *Live At The Fillmore East*.) But its leanings towards a rock/funk crossover indicated at least one of the musical directions he'd been exploring in recent months, and the recruitment of his first all-black band since he'd met Chas Chandler did improve his standing among radical activists such as The Black Panthers.

Band Of Gypsys

(Version 1)

LP release: Polydor/Track 2406 002 (USA), June 1970
CD release: Polydor 821 933-2 (Germany), May 1988

TRACKS: Who Knows/Machine Gun/Changes/Power To Love/Message Of Love/We Gotta Live Together

THE ORIGINAL POLYDOR CD RELEASE WAS TYPICAL OF THEIR LACK OF ATTENTION to detail: the sound quality was murky, and the credits suggested that all six songs had been recorded on December 31, 1969, whereas they actually came from the following day's shows – 'Who Knows' and 'Machine Gun' from the opening set, the rest from the second house.

Students of the macabre might consider tracking down the Japanese CD edition of *Band Of Gypsys* (Polydor P20P-22006) as this uses the original 'puppet' cover (depicting Jimi with friends including the late Brian Jones, and DJ John Peel) prepared for the first pressing of the UK LP in 1970. Pressure from Mike Jeffery forced Track Records to alter the artwork later that year, but nobody told the Japanese.

Band Of Gypsys

(Version 2)

CD release: Polydor 847 237-2 (Germany), 1993

TRACKS: Who Knows/Machine Gun/Changes/Power Of Love/Message To Love/We Gotta Live Together/Hear My Train A-Comin'/Foxy Lady/Stop

IN 1986, ALAN DOUGLAS ISSUED *BAND OF GYPSYS 2*, A MISBEGOTTEN VINYL-ONLY release that never appeared outside America. In fact, two versions of this LP were released, albeit with identical cover artwork, making it impossible to distinguish between them at first glance.

The major problem with Douglas' creation was that only three of the tracks from the album actually featured the Band Of Gypsys: the rest came from Berkeley and Atlanta shows in 1970, with the revamped Experience.

In 1991, the three authentic BOG songs were added to the original six when the CD was included in the *Footlights* boxed set. Meanwhile, the six-song edition remained in the shops. In 1992, Douglas explained that the revamped *Band Of Gypsys* wasn't available separately because he wanted to change it again: "I found four more new tracks. We have three that have never been released, including a very good 'Stepping Stone', and we have all four 'Machine Guns'. I'm trying to get Capitol to sit down and forget everything that's happened and we'll pick the best tracks and make the best of it."

What happened next? In 1993, the 1991 edition of *Band Of Gypsys* appeared on CD in its own right, with the ridiculous claim that it "contains 3 previously unreleased tracks". No 'Stepping Stone', no new 'Machine Gun'; just more egg on the Estate's collective face. To compound the mistakes, the titles of two of the songs were mistakenly altered; and a third was listed with the wrong composer.

Meanwhile, in the USA, Capitol returned to the album – and reissued not the updated and extended version that Douglas had looked forward to, but the original six-track edition. They claimed that the dense legal red-tape surrounding the project left them no choice. The bad karma surrounding *Band Of Gypsys* continued.

Band Of Gypsys

(Version 3)

MCA MCD 11607 (UK), April 1997

TRACKS: Who Knows/Machine Gun/Changes/Power Of Love/Message To Love/We Gotta Live Together

THE TRACK LISTING MAY HAVE REMAINED UNCHANGED FROM THE ORIGINAL, but the superb packaging of this set lent the album a long-overdue sense of dignity. John McDermott's lengthy liner notes explained the circumstances surrounding the band, the concerts and the Chalpin/Capitol debacle without being judgmental about any of the participants.

WHO KNOWS

WITH THE Band Of Gypsys, Jimi had to balance the energetic enthusiasm of Buddy Miles' playing against his tendency to turn every song into a call-and-response routine with the audience. The mid-tempo solidity of 'Who Knows' – more a groove than a song – typified the fluency of Hendrix's playing at these shows, and the low level of inspiration involved in some of the composing. But most of all it demonstrated the chasm that sometimes opened between Jimi's soul and Buddy's showbiz – one self-effacing, the other almost exhibitionistic.

MACHINE GUN

WHETHER you regarded it as a comment on the Vietnam conflict, or a wider outburst of grief and anger at the racial divide, 'Machine Gun' inspired some of Hendrix's most majestic and anguished guitar work throughout the Fillmore shows. Note after sustained note was mutated into a deathly, screaming howl, while Miles brought a martial air to his drum patterns, and Billy Cox toyed with a bass riff similar to Cream's 'Sunshine Of Your Love'. Like 'Hear My Train A-Comin'' before it, 'Machine Gun' became a failsafe connection to Hendrix's muse during the final year of his life. This Fillmore East performance alone would have legitimised the very existence of the Band Of Gypsys.

CHANGES

SOMETIMES known as 'Them Changes', this was the first of Miles' songs on the album – little more than a lightweight Stax R&B riff, to be honest, topped with a melody line that stretched Buddy's voice to the limit. Jimi's chief involvement was layering wah-wah guitar across the chorus and contributing a spunky solo. Miles' later studio recording of 'Them Changes' provided him with a small hit single around the time that *Band Of Gypsys* was released.

POWER OF SOUL

IT WAS listed as 'Power To Love' on the first and last CD editions, 'Power Of Love' on the second, 'With The Power' on a later compilation, and often introduced in concert by Jimi as either 'Crash Landing' or 'Paper Airplanes'. But the 'correct' title came from the chorus line, which sums up the song's message: "with the power of soul/anything is possible". Deliberately understated, the song downplayed Hendrix's trademark guitar theatrics in favour of a series of tight, circular funk riffs, closely echoed by the melody line. Miles and Hendrix reached back into their R&B apprenticeship for the slightly awkward interlocking vocals, before the performance stumbled to a halt.

MESSAGE TO LOVE

THIS SONG also went through a change of title: it was listed on the first CD release as 'Message Of Love', and it had its origins in a piece entitled 'Message To The Universe'. Its theme was the same as its predecessor, but it lacked the subtle touch of 'Power Of Soul', and never really broke out of its vague funk origins to become a fully-fledged song. Hendrix's riffing was altogether more convincing, however, looking ahead to the funk-edged fluency that he would later bring to 'Freedom'.

WE GOTTA LIVE TOGETHER

HENDRIX gifted this second Buddy Miles tune (again, later a minor hit for its composer) with some astonishing guitar playing, as free-flowing and ambitious as anything on the album. But like too much of *Band Of Gypsys*, the song was a genre exercise in funk-soul, rather than a composition that boasted any unique reason for its existence. This edited mix – the whole thing can be tasted on *Live At The Fillmore East* – brought the album to a downbeat close.

SECTION 2
THE POSTHUMOUS ALBUMS

JIMI HENDRIX'S FINAL DAY IN NEW YORK CLIMAXED WITH THE OFFICIAL OPENING of his Electric Lady Studios. He left the party early; he never entered a studio again. His final recording, a fragment entitled 'Slow Blues,' ended abruptly – a prophetic glimpse of what was to follow.

Two days later, on 28 August 1970, Jimi Hendrix gave an interview to *Melody Maker* journalist Roy Hollingworth. "I've given this era of music everything," he said. "I still sound the same, my music's the same, and I can't think of anything new to add to it in its present state. This era of music, sparked off by The Beatles, has come to an end. Something new has got to come and Jimi Hendrix will be there.

"I want a big band. I don't mean three harps and fourteen violins. I mean a big band full of competent musicians that I can conduct and write for. And with the music we will paint pictures of earth and space, so that the listener can be taken somewhere."

Three weeks later, Hendrix was dead. He left behind him scores of tape reels, stuffed full of jams, half-finished masters, demos, jokes, sketches for compositions in progress, layers of interlocked guitar overdubs. On paper and on tape, he'd laid out the skeleton of an autobiographical song cycle called *Black Gold*. More openly, he had spoken to many of his friends and associates about plans for his next album, a double-LP to be called *The First Rays Of The New Rising Sun*.

It was never completed; neither was *Black Gold*. But Hendrix's career as a posthumous recording star was just beginning. His death was the signal for everyone who owned a piece of studio tape bearing his music to cash in their chips. For the next five years, the market was flooded with unauthorised albums, carrying similar material to the 'Unofficial CDs' covered elsewhere in this book.

Those worthless exercises in exploitation queered the pitch for the 'official' Hendrix release schedule, which began just a few weeks after Jimi's demise, paused briefly in the late Seventies, and then gradually picked up steam after 1980. In the immediate aftermath of his death, there was an insistent demand for 'new' Hendrix product. His first posthumous album came close to topping the British and American charts, while the uncompromisingly brilliant guitar extravaganza that was 'Voodoo Child (Slight Return)' actually reached No. 1 on the UK singles chart in the final weeks of 1970.

But very quickly the law of diminishing returns assumed command, both commercially and artistically. By the mid-Seventies, the audience for the increasingly unsatisfactory albums being issued under Hendrix's name was rapidly disintegrating into a vocal core of fanatics who began to swap concert tapes and dream that one day *Black Gold* would magically be transformed from myth into reality.

The final straw for many Hendrix followers was the overdubbing of his original tapes for two mid-Seventies albums – not simply because his tracks were being tampered with, but because project supremo Alan Douglas had chosen not to use Jimi's original sidemen to carry out the repairs.

Douglas, who had worked with Hendrix on several musical concepts in 1969 and 1970, gradually assumed command over Jimi's entire catalogue, however. After one more dip into the treasure-house of unissued tapes in 1980, he spent the next few years preparing a series of compilations, decorated with the minimum of unheard live material. The late-Eighties release of albums like *Live At Winterland* and *Radio One* denoted a new openness in his philosophy, but even the most spectacular of Douglas' releases fell short of finding universal acceptance. Fans still demanded the impossible; Douglas presented them with naked commercial regard, sometimes presented as altruism.

The emergence of a new regime, named Experience Hendrix, in January 1997, reopened all the debates that Douglas hoped he had closed.

Just as Douglas had done with *Voodoo Soup* in 1995, Experience Hendrix attempted to create a definitive version of the album on which Jimi had been working at his death. In addition, they set about a rigorous campaign of tape research, under the control of Jimi's original engineer, Eddie Kramer. "You can bet your bottom dollar that there's going to be some very interesting stuff coming out," Kramer promised as the new regime took over, "stuff that's never seen the light of day, not even on bootlegs. Quite frankly, if it's good, it'll see the light of day. If it's crap, it won't. We want to make sure that when we do put stuff out, it has meaning and is of decent quality." By and large, Experience Hendrix have kept this promise – both with the releases detailed below, and with the deliberately less commercial CDs on the Dagger label, which are listed elsewhere in this book.

THE NEW HENDRIX CATALOGUE:

STUDIO ALBUMS

The First Rays Of The New Rising Sun

MCA 11599 (UK), April 1997

FOR THE FINAL TWO YEARS OF HIS LIFE, JIMI HENDRIX BATTLED AGAINST HIS OWN creativity and indecisiveness. His quest was to complete a studio album that could live up to the majesty and ambition of *Electric Ladyland*. His problems were the sheer quantity of material that he was recording, and his inability to fix on a single vehicle or approach for his work.

In retrospect, it's clear that this troubled period of Hendrix's life was every bit as productive as the two remarkable years that had preceded it. From the autumn of 1968 until his death, he wrote, rewrote and recorded at a phenomenal rate. The result was hundreds of hours of tapes, varying from free-form jams to meticulously overdubbed studio masters. During this period, he experimented with a series of different musical line-ups, from the Experience, through the extended Gypsy, Sun & Rainbows that performed at the Woodstock festival, and the Band Of Gypsys, to the basic three-piece group featuring Mitch Mitchell and Billy Cox with whom he played his final shows.

Along the way, his concept for the unfinished album went through an equally diverse set of changes. There was talk of a single album, or a double, or maybe even a triple, perhaps called *People, Hell & Angels. Straight Ahead* was one title that constantly recurred. But the name to which Jimi returned most often was *(The) First Rays Of The (New) Rising Sun*. Shortly before his death, he sketched out a track listing for – frustratingly – three of the four sides of a double-LP under that title. Despite his massive backlog of studio work, he still regarded the majority of the proposed inclusions as unfinished.

Jimi's provisional track listing ran as follows:
SIDE A: Dolly Dagger/Night Bird Flying/Room Full Of Mirrors/Belly Button Window/Freedom.

SIDE B: Ezy Ryder/Astro Man/Drifting/Straight Ahead.
SIDE C: Drifter's Escape/Comin' Down Hard On Me/Beginnings/Cherokee Mist/Angel." Other songs judged to be under consideration for the album's final side include 'Hey Baby (Land Of The New Rising Sun)', 'Country Blues', 'Pali Gap', 'Just Came In (From The Storm)', 'Lover Man' and 'Valleys Of Neptune'.

Faced with the need to compile an album immediately after Hendrix's death in 1970, Eddie Kramer selected nine of these songs, plus the *Electric Ladyland* out-take 'My Friend'. The result was *The Cry Of Love*, accepted for years as an authentic Hendrix album rather than a posthumous compilation. Then, in 1994, Alan Douglas announced plans to replace Kramer's concoction with an album titled *First Rays Of The New Rising Sun*, with the contents chosen by Hendrix's fans. Instead, he released *Voodoo Soup* the following year, which used just seven *Cry Of Love* songs.

With Kramer back in joint command after 1997, he had the opportunity for a slightly more considered shot at translating Hendrix's final wishes into reality. Not surprisingly, his track listing included the entire contents of *The Cry Of Love* – plus, so Kramer explained, "all of the songs that he was working on at that particular time, which he had designed for that album".

The project was advertised as "The music the way (Jimi) intended it … the album Jimi would have released, had he lived to complete it." "The problem," Hendrix scholar and Estate archivist John McDermott told *ICE* magazine, "is that the mixes were changed by the previous administration to try to create something different from what had been *The Cry Of Love*. With *First Rays*, what we tried to do with Eddie Kramer is look solely at the songs that Jimi wanted for that double album."

Careful comparison of Hendrix's track listing above, and the contents of the eventual CD below, will reveal many differences. So the *First Rays* CD is no more a 'definitive' version of Jimi's final wishes than *Voodoo Soup* or indeed *The Cry Of Love*. On its own terms, however, it emerged as a worthy tribute to Hendrix's art – and an illustration of the chaos in which he left his catalogue.

FREEDOM

NONE OF Hendrix's studio versions of this song ever matched the spectacular guitar theatrics or sheer spirit of liberation heard when he played it at the Isle Of Wight Festival in August 1970. Jimi had worked on the song sporadical- ly over the previous three months at Electric Lady Studios, with the Mitchell/Cox rhythm section joined by the Ghetto Fighters vocal duo and percussionist Juma Sultan. Its lyrical theme was not just political but romantic, with a chilling reference to his girlfriend's heroin addiction in the first verse (widely quoted as referring to Devon Wilson).

Kramer's remix of this fiery, almost orchestrated piece of rock-funk retained the triple-guitar overdubs originally heard on *The Cry Of Love*, but with digitally enhanced clarity and impact.

IZABELLA

TIGHTLY wound and intense, 'Izabella' emerged from the *Band Of Gypsys* sessions of January 1970, was briefly available as a single that spring, and then overdubbed in June 1970. During that process, Mitch Mitchell replaced Buddy Miles' original drum track.

The song was written from the perspective of a soldier adrift from his family, presumably in Vietnam: "soon I'll be holding you instead of this machine gun". For the first time, Hendrix referred to "the rays of the new rising sun", but here they signified it was time for conflict, rather than spiritual rebirth as elsewhere in his work.

NIGHT BIRD FLYING

THIS BEAUTIFUL merging of romance and Eros was inspired by late night DJ Alison Steele, billed as 'The Nightbird', on New York radio station WNEW. It built on the foundations of a piece called 'Ships Passing Through The Night', introduced into Hendrix's repertoire in 1968. Kramer's 1997 mix simply enhanced the soundscape he'd prepared in 1970 for *The Cry Of Love*.

ANGEL

WRITTEN by the end of 1967, yet strangely not considered for *Electric Ladyland*, this gorgeous ballad has become a rock standard, thanks in part to a superlative cover by Rod Stewart in 1972. It was apparently inspired by a dream about his mother, which maybe explained his desire to hold the song back until it was absolutely perfect. Certainly in August 1970 he regarded it as still "unfinished". Mitch Mitchell did his best to correct that, adding another layer of percussion overdubs in October 1970 that were accentuated in Kramer's mix for this album. On The Cry Of Love, Jimi's vocal was shadowy and deep in the mix; here it was pushed closer to the front of the sonic picture.

ROOM FULL OF MIRRORS

LIKE MANY of Hendrix's original songs, 'Room Full Of Mirrors' grew out of his obsession with the Delta blues, eventually taking on a discreet structure of its own. Its initial theme of fear and loathing gave way to a hint of redemption by the final verse, though the heavily overdubbed, pressurised performance (taped between November 1969 and August 1970) emphasised the eerier of the two themes. *The First Rays* version heightened that effect by leaving the bass and percussion high in the mix: the result was funk first, psychedelia very much second.

DOLLY DAGGER

"WATCH out Devon", Jimi called during this performance, leaving no doubt about the identity of his muse for this strident, dark funk tune. Although he warned that "she drinks the blood from a jagged edge", making her sound like a savage succubus, the performance was filled with a playful sense of affection. Taped in July/August 1970, this was originally planned by Hendrix for single release later that year, but first emerged instead on *Rainbow Bridge*.

EZY RYDER

THOUGH an occasional air of hope fought its way through the multi-layered guitars of this uptempo funk-rock anthem, the dominant atmosphere was doomladen: "He's talking about dying, he's so tragic baby … How long do you think he's gonna last?" It wasn't just Hendrix's death that raised the question of whether he was singing about himself. The song obviously tantalised him, as he first attempted it during the Band Of Gypsys' sessions in December 1969, and tinkered with it until shortly before his death.

DRIFTING

THREE generations of this splendidly minimal tune attempted to capture the spirit of the title in the vocal mix. On *The Cry Of Love*, Jimi's voice was left to float in the breeze; on *Voodoo Soup*, it entered a cave of echo; finally, on *First Rays*, it received a more natural but grounded production. Sonically, this was Hendrix's successor to the sublime 'Little Wing', with his guitar squeezed through a Leslie speaker and Buzzy Linhart adding delicate touches of vibes a few weeks after Jimi's death.

BEGINNINGS

OTHERWISE known as 'Beginning' (on *War Heroes*) or 'Jam Back At The House' (*Live At Woodstock*), this was a bubbling cauldron of rock and funk, with obvious links to such Experience stage favourites as 'Drivin' South' and 'Killing Floor'. It was taped on 1 July, 1970 and then revisited at one of Jimi's final sessions in August.

STEPPING STONE

IN 1967, 'Fire' was Hendrix's take on the prevailing sound of Stax R&B. Three years later, with funk to the fore, 'Stepping Stone' occupied an equivalent space. No fewer than four separate mixes of this frantic tune have been released down the years, three of them – this one included – featuring Mitch Mitchell's overdubbed drum parts. A few seconds of ambient noise at the opening of this track were revealed here for the first time, while Eddie Kramer chose to retain an additional guitar part in the intro that received its debut exposure on Alan Douglas' *Voodoo Soup* set.

MY FRIEND

NEWLY arrived in New York in March 1968, Hendrix was keen to party and to experiment in the studio, and both callings coincided on this recording. It had nothing to do with the *First Rays* concept and might have been better suited to the subsequent *South Saturn Delta* album. But its Dylan-esque lyrics (someone even crooned a line from 'Blowin' In The Wind' over the fade-out) and hedonistic feel made it irresistibly attractive – which is no doubt why it was exhumed for *The Cry Of Love* in 1970. "I just got out of a Scandinavian jail", Jimi boasted of his recent bust, while friends such as Paul Caruso, Ken Pine, Jimmy Mayes and (for a few seconds) Stephen Stills romped behind him.

STRAIGHT AHEAD

FOR A WHILE, *Straight Ahead* was strongly considered by Hendrix as a potential title for his 1970 studio album. Originally titled 'Pass It On', the song of that name was recorded that summer as an activist anthem: "Power to the people, that's what they're spieling, freedom of the soul, pass it on, pass it on to the young and old". What sounded muted, verging on dead, on *The Cry Of Love* was transformed on *First Rays* into a thrilling variation on the 'Freedom' template.

HEY BABY
(NEW RISING SUN)

ON 'IZABELLA', the new rising sun was a threat; here it was a promise, of both romantic and spiritual nature, as this live-in-the-studio exploration from 1 July, 1970 slowly developed into a coherent song. Hendrix clearly didn't consider this a master – "is the microphone on?" he asked midway through – but the centrality of the lyric to his concept for the album meant that this begged to be rescued from obscurity on the long-lost *Rainbow Bridge* LP.

EARTH BLUES

HENDRIX rarely exposed himself too nakedly in his lyrics, and 'Earth Blues' carefully combined political and gospel motifs, while only hinting ("Don't get too stoned, please remember you're a man") at a more personal subtext. Either way, this was a stunning performance, originally cut when Jimi was considering a Band Of Gypsys studio album, overdubbed with strident backing vocals by The Ronettes (of 'Be My Baby' fame), and then adjusted in June 1970 with Mitch Mitchell on drums and more layers of Hendrix guitars. In this final guise, it was originally aired on *Rainbow Bridge*.

ASTRO MAN

THE KID in Jimi loved DC and Marvel comics. Hence the invented superheroes whose names he affixed to the manuscript for this song: "Astro Man & Strato-Woman: The Cosmic Lovers Of The Universe & everything". In the studio, he even imagined a TV theme tune for Astro Man's adventures. What emerged on record, originally included on *The Cry Of Love* in 1970, was this joyous piece of modern blues mythology, which ended with a spiralling guitar figure as our hero headed for the skies.

IN FROM THE STORM

HENDRIX called this tune 'Just Came In', and its dignified, magisterial quality made it a poignant closing number for his tempestuous performance at the Isle of Wight. With hints of both 'Gypsy Eyes' and 'Freedom' in its construction, it was built around a killer riff and a deep blues sensibility. The original mix of this summer 1970 recording, prepared for *The Cry Of Love*, left the vocal frail and distant, as if the storm was about to carry him away. Eddie Kramer pulled Jimi much higher in the mix on this, his second attempt, some 16 years later.

BELLY BUTTON WINDOW

BASSIST Billy Cox recalled that this tune was inspired by Jimi's discovery that Mitch Mitchell's wife, Lynn, was pregnant. In his fertile imagination, he concocted this monologue for the unborn child, who veered back and forth from vulnerability to a hint of malevolence during the course of the lyric. The baby-to-be was left searching somewhat fruitlessly for a reason to enter the world – a theme seized upon after Jimi's death by those who alleged he had committed suicide.

Hendrix, Cox and Mitchell first ran through the song during a July 1970 session, but it was a month later that Jimi taped this solo demo. On *The Cry Of Love*, Eddie Kramer prepared a suitably womb-like mix, but the *First Rays* revamp allowed the child closer to the outside world.

South Saturn Delta

MCA 11684 (UK), October 1997

TO FORESTALL ANY CRITICISM ABOUT THE TRACK SELECTION OF *FIRST RAYS OF The New Rising Sun*, Experience Hendrix quickly followed through with this random assembly of studio out-takes. The contents spanned three years and a multitude of different Hendrix projects. As co-compiler John McDermott explained, the project was meant to be expansive: "These fifteen diverse recordings provide a unique window into one of the most fertile minds in the history of popular music".

LOOK OVER YONDER

EVEN BEFORE the formation of the Experience, Hendrix was performing this song, known then as 'Mr. Bad Luck'. After a second fleeting incarnation as 'Mr. Lost Soul', it assumed its final form – a virtual cross between 'Stone Free' and 'House Burning Down', which updated some old blues clichés about the devil along the way. The October 1968 session tape was drastically remixed by Eddie Kramer, John Jansen and Mitch Mitchell in May 1971, resulting in one of Hendrix's most anonymous vocals becoming virtually lost in the swirl of stereo panning. It was rescued for this project from the *Rainbow Bridge* album.

LITTLE WING

I GNORE the title, which is what was on the tape box: what Jimi and Mitch Mitchell recorded at Olympic Studios in October 1967 wasn't the familiar *Axis* ballad, but the first instrumental sketch for the equally beautiful 'Angel'. The precise structure had yet to be perfected, but the skeleton of the song was already in place.

HERE HE COMES (LOVER MAN)

THE JIMI Hendrix Experience set documented the first rising of this revamp of the blues standard 'Rock Me Baby', in 1967. In October 1968, the Experience tried again, opening with ferocious rhythm patterns before Hendrix – on magnificent form – led his surprisingly sluggish rhythm section through six minutes of jamming, scat-singing to fill out the time.

SOUTH SATURN DELTA

TWO SESSIONS at the Record Plant in New York, from May and June 1969, produced this fascinating instrumental sketch for a merger between a funk trio and a horn band (the latter directed by Larry

Fallon). The two elements never quite meshed, but this was still an intriguing suggestion of a possible direction that Hendrix never really followed through.

POWER OF SOUL

THIS FAMILIAR Band Of Gypsys tune was still known as 'Paper Airplanes' when the trio attempted a studio version in January/February 1970. Like so many BOG performances, it was overdubbed that August but then rejected for consideration when Jimi was planning the contents of his next studio album that month. Filled with interlocking guitar parts, it lacked the directness of the live version on *Band Of Gypsys*. This performance was overdubbed posthumously at Alan Douglas's command for the *Crash Landing* album.

MESSAGE TO THE UNIVERSE (MESSAGE TO LOVE)

BEFORE the band became a trio, Jimi, Billy Cox and Buddy Miles operated during the late summer of 1969 as a six-piece, with Jerry Velez and Juma Sultan on percussion, and Larry Lee on second guitar. This was the debut studio outing for the line-up that performed at Woodstock, revisiting their opening number in less focused form.

TAX FREE

BO HANSSON and Jan Carlsson's march tune was a favourite jam-ming vehicle for the Experience in 1968 and 1969. This studio rendition was an early candidate for Electric Ladyland, eventually losing its place to more fluid and less structured sources of improvisation. After the initial January 1968 session in London, Jimi added a rhythm guitar part played through a Leslie organ speaker in New York. The finished track first appeared on the *War Heroes* LP.

ALL ALONG THE WATCHTOWER

NOT THE single, but a stepping stone to the same: this work-in-progress mix from January 21, 1968 lacked the production finesse of the final version, sounding strangely flat by comparison. But as a historical document it had its moments, especially in the way it exposed Dave Mason's acoustic 12-string strumming.

THE STARS THAT PLAY WITH LAUGHING SAM'S DICE

THE B-SIDE of 'The Burning Of The Midnight Lamp' was a sonic adventure from the start – nega-tively so in the case of the appalling-ly muddy mix that was included on the original *Smash Hits* CD in the Eighties. Meanwhile, John Jansen and Eddie Kramer remixed the tune for inclusion on *Loose Ends* in the early Seventies, and it was that ver-sion that got souped up digitally for this release. The result was easily the finest ever presentation of the song, a joyous cacophony of psychedelia and studio madness.

MIDNIGHT

LIKE A slower remake of 'Purple Haze', this tune emerged from the final set of Experience studio recordings in April 1969. It was little more than a structure around which Jimi could wail on guitar – an instrumental recording first aired on *War Heroes*.

SWEET ANGEL (ANGEL)

SECOND time around, 'Angel' still bore a title-in-progress. A month after the taping of the Jimi/Mitch demo heard earlier on this set, Jimi prepared this solo demo, using guitar, bass and an endearingly primitive drum machine. He took the song slightly too fast, but in this form it was complete – making it all the more remarkable that it was never released in his lifetime.

BLEEDING HEART

HENDRIX applied just enough originality to this blues standard by Elmore James that he could eventually claim the writing credit as his own – not that he released the song during his lifetime. This rendition, taped by the Hendrix/Cox/Mitchell trio in March and June 1970, was selected for the *War Heroes* LP. His overdubbed guitar parts carried the chattering, insistent funk sound typical of his final experiments in the studio.

PALI GAP

HENDRIX's manager, Mike Jeffery, provided a Hawaiian name for this instrumental, when he was concocting *Rainbow Bridge* as a supposed soundtrack for the movie of Jimi's adventures on that island. In Jimi's lifetime, it was known more prosaically as 'Slow Part', having emerged from a July 1, 1970 jam from 'Dolly Dagger' into 'Gimme Some Lovin'. Built around a simple three-chord pattern, it was transformed into a Grateful Dead-like musical excursion when Jimi applied multiple guitar overdubs.

DRIFTER'S ESCAPE

HIS PERENNIAL fascination with Bob Dylan's songwriting led Hendrix to experiment with a series of Dylan tunes between 1967, among them 'Like A Rolling Stone' and 'Tears Of Rage'. 'All Along The Watchtower' was the most significant of these adventures, of course, and 'Drifter's Escape' was Jimi's attempt to duplicate its impact. Instead, as this alternate take of the version released on Loose Ends exemplified, he had begun to lose his way during his 1970 sessions, cluttering his recordings with surplus guitar parts and sacrificing the emotional intensity that was his greatest strength.

MIDNIGHT LIGHTNING

THE CONTRAST between the previous track and this finale could hardly have been more pronounced. After the sonic excess of 'Drifter's Escape', here was an entirely solo performance from March 23, 1970, with Jimi tapping his foot on the floor as he laid down this blues-tinged demo. Delicate and haunting, this conveyed far more of Hendrix's musical spirit than the overdubbed rendition of the same song which became the title track of a posthumous album.

The Jimi Hendrix Experience

MCA 805-112-316-2 (UK), September 2000

RATHER THAN PARCEL OUT HENDRIX'S OUT-TAKES INTO A SERIES OF THEMED albums, Experience Hendrix chose to compile this career-spanning 4-CD box set (so-called, but actually a book-format package with a detailed booklet). It represented an alternate history of his progress from 1966 to 1970, taking in different versions of familiar songs, studio out-takes, jam sessions, and some of the most significant live recordings that had slipped out of print over the previous two decades. Purists argued that the title (and indeed cover art) was slightly misleading, as the set strayed way beyond the joint escapades of Jimi's original trio. But that was the only possible criticism of a magnificent piece of archive work, recommended to anyone remotely intrigued by Hendrix's music.

CD1

PURPLE HAZE

A SUBTLY different take of Hendrix's classic account of psychedelic dislocation provided a suitably intriguing introduction to the set. Prepared at Olympic Studios in February 1967, it featured a notably flatter production sound than the single, a less processed and indeed precise lead vocal, and background voices that called from beyond the grave.

KILLING FLOOR/HEY JOE

A WEEK before they recorded together for the first time, the Experience were at the Olympia in Paris, supporting local superstar Johnny Hallyday. As these two excerpts from their fourth ever gig (October 18, 1966) proved, the trio were already locked onto each other's wavelengths. 'Killing Floor' was spectacular, with Mitch Mitchell fully focused on his new role, and Hendrix soloing like the blues showman he'd recently been. 'Hey Joe' was more erratic, speeding and slowing like a car driven by over-excited kids, but the ecstatic reception from the Parisian crowd proved that even before they had issued their first single, the Experience had real stage presence.

FOXY LADY

LIKE 'PURPLE HAZE', this December 1966 out-take from CBS Studios offered a game of spot-the-difference from the familiar master. With its eerily compressed lead vocal and whispered responses, 'Foxy Lady' offered sonic novelty even before the sliding effects of the finale.

HIGHWAY CHILE

FOR THE first time, the box set offered the B-side of 'The Wind Cries Mary' in true stereo, and unedited to the extent that it ended in a few seconds of studio chatter.

HEY JOE

IN AN attempt to perfect Jimi's debut single, producer Chas Chandler dragged his protégé around a succession of London studios in October 1966. Here was one of the stops they made at Pye Studios, with Hendrix obviously distracted by the overly dramatic background vocals – subsequently replaced for the final release.

TITLE #3

HENDRIX'S studio catalogue is replete with untitled jams, but this April 1967 out-take from the *Are You Experienced* sessions was a structured slice of psychedelic R&B – patently a backing track for an unknown song rather than a piece of collective musical exploration.

THIRD STONE FROM THE SUN

HYSTERIA soon set in as Hendrix and Chandler attempted to

overdub the sci-fi dialogue intended to accompany this space-age instrumental. This audio-verite` tape illustrated their mutual affection, and led into a subtly remixed version of the finished track – revealing that the lines which had caused them so much trouble were destined to become incomprehensible to anyone whose ears worked at normal human speed.

TAKING CARE OF NO BUSINESS

CLOSER to vaudeville than psychedelia, 'Taking Care Of No Business' caught Hendrix at his most comedic, hamming his way through a shaggy dog tale at Olympic Studios in May 1967. Mitch Mitchell's tambourine was his only accompaniment, beyond the staged dialogue that opened the track. The box set featured the original mix, before the subsequent addition of a tuba overdub.

HERE HE COMES (LOVER MAN)

NOT FOR the first time, Jimi borrowed an R&B standard – B.B. King's 'Rock Me Baby' – as the skeleton for this tune. Presented here in purely instrumental form, the similarities between the two were glaring. Three years after cutting this out-take at Olympic in April 1967 Hendrix was still trying unsuccessfully to document a definitive studio version of the song.

THE BURNING OF THE MIDNIGHT LAMP

CONVINCED that harpsichord was the ideal setting for this song, Jimi steered the Experience through this trial run, hammering the instrument like Jerry Lee Lewis. Mitch Mitchell responded in kind, and if this arrangement had survived for longer than a one-verse run-through, 'Midnight Lamp' might never have made it onto record.

IF SIX WAS NINE

A PLAYGROUND for anoraks: a mono mix of the completed counter-culture anthem from the *Axis* album, with different aural effects and additional background vocals that were deleted from the finished track.

ROCK ME BABY/ LIKE A ROLLING STONE

THE EXPERIENCE'S scene-stealing performance at the Monterey International Pop Festival on 18 June, 1967 was a landmark in Hendrix's acceptance in his homeland. Remixed from the long-deleted CD of the entire show, with the guitar louder and thicker in the mix than before, this brace of tracks provided California's hippest audience with a primer in where Hendrix had learned his craft (the blues and Dylan) and where he was headed (the outer reaches of the imagination).

CD2

SGT. PEPPER'S LONELY HEARTS CLUB BAND/ THE BURNING OF THE MIDNIGHT LAMP

A S HEARD briefly on the CD box set Stages, these were the opening two numbers of the Experience's show in a Stockholm radio studio on 5 September, 1967. After a slightly shambolic tribute to The Beatles, there was the live debut of 'Midnight Lamp' – understandably hesitant, but still playful, with Jimi adding a deliberate discord to the end of the guitar intro.

LITTLE WING

PERHAPS the most delicate and beautiful of Hendrix's ballads, 'Little Wing' was originally attempted in more robust style, as this instrumental run-through from Olympic in October 1967 demonstrated. The subsequent reduction in intensity was undoubtedly a smart move, but this passionate and powerful performance had a majesty of its own.

LITTLE MISS LOVER

WITH LESS dramatic phasing and stereo panning, this *Axis* outtake offered a minor variation on the familiar LP version.

THE WIND CRIES MARY/ CATFISH BLUES

HENDRIX had clearly not forgotten the exuberance of his October 1966 reception at the Paris Olympia, as his grateful comments from his return a year later revealed. After a very straight rendition of their recent single, the trio explored their debt to Muddy Waters' delta blues, as Jimi promised, "our own way, the Experience way". Blues purists would have approved, at least until the Mississippi became a raging torrent as Jimi powered into an explosive guitar solo.

BOLD AS LOVE

DOCUMENTED on the tape box as 'Version II Title X', this was a beautifully weighted backing track for one of the highlights of the *Axis* album, lacking any of the phasing trickery heard on the finished version.

SWEET ANGEL

ALMOST three years before he recorded his final (though still unfinished) version of 'Angel', Hendrix debuted the tune on solo guitar to the surreal accompaniment of a primitive drum machine.

Recorded immediately after the completion of the *Axis* album in November 1967, this track was subsequently overdubbed (as heard on *South Saturn Delta*) and then quietly abandoned.

FIRE

AS A TASTER for the Dagger Records series of CDs, the box set offered this excerpt from *Live At Clark University* – a March 1968 stomp through a concert stalwart.

SOMEWHERE

ORIGINALLY nothing more than a demo for a song briefly under consideration for *Electric Ladyland*, this recording was overdubbed by Mitch Mitchell after Hendrix's death, and then reworked by Alan Douglas' team for the controversial *Crash Landing* album. The undubbed demo was presumably lost in action, as the box set included the intermediate version with Mitchell's additions.

HAVE YOU EVER BEEN (TO ELECTRIC LADYLAND)?

DEBUTED but long forgotten on the *Loose Ends* album from the early Seventies, this delicious piece of Curtis Mayfield-inspired soul was a worthy revival on the box set. Mitch Mitchell's original drumming was removed to reveal the unadorned beauty of Hendrix's guitar, en route to creating the title track of his finest album.

GYPSY EYES

SEVEN hours of mixing were required to produce this rendition of the *Electric Ladyland* classic, which Hendrix duly rejected as failing to match his dreams. Notable differences from the album mix included striking variations in the use of phasing, and more overt double-tracking.

ROOM FULL OF MIRRORS

LIKE 'ANGEL', 'Room Full Of Mirrors' remained high on Hendrix's priorities for the remainder of his life. This August 1968 demo marked the beginning of the saga, with Jimi's solo guitar and Paul Caruso's harp providing an authentic Delta blues feel.

GLORIA

VAN MORRISON'S 1964 composition became a staple among virtually every Sixties R&B and garage band, and the Experience clearly relished this October 1968 romp through its trademark three chords. The track was first exposed on *The Essential Jimi Hendrix*, but this was the full, virtually nine-minute take. While Hendrix coaxed a flood of noise out of his guitar, and Noel Redding sparked comparisons with the Who's John Entwistle, Mitch Mitchell was left slightly at sea by the simplicity of the song's structure, a rare lapse from his usual perfection in the studio. Hence, perhaps, Jimi's decision to lampoon his drummer's sexual adventures, before he moved on to target Redding in the interests of fair play.

IT'S TOO BAD

RACIAL and family politics were the twin themes of this earnest blues performance from February 1969, which teamed Hendrix with organist Larry Young and future Band Of Gypsys drummer, Buddy Miles. Jimi rarely exposed himself so openly, even in the privacy of the studio, and this cut would never have been released if he had lived, regardless of its musical merits.

STAR SPANGLED BANNER

NOTHING could have been further removed from the anguished intensity of Jimi's Woodstock rendition of the American national anthem than this multi-dubbed studio concoction, taped during his first ever 16-track session in March 1969. Originally included on the *Rainbow Bridge* LP, it sounded like banal self-parody; but with hindsight, what was maybe more important was the verve of Hendrix's attempt to create synthesised sound without a computer.

CD3

STONE FREE

AMERICA had missed out on the original 1966 recording of 'Stone Free', and the imminent release there of the *Smash Hits* collection presumably prompted Jimi to return to the tune at the Record Plant in April 1969. This track, featuring guest vocals from Roger Chapman (Family) and Andy Fairweather-Low (Amen Corner), was originally released in over-dubbed form on *Crash Landing* – but this release returned to the version Jimi actually recorded.

SPANISH CASTLE MAGIC/HEAR MY TRAIN A-COMIN'

A SERIES of Olympic Studios sessions by the Experience during February 1969 produced virtually nothing of value – save a series of rehearsals on the 17th, the day before the trio's first show at the Royal Albert Hall. Running through their live set without an audience, Hendrix, Redding and Mitchell cut flawless renditions of two of their concert showcases, the extended 'Spanish Castle Magic' and arguably Jimi's finest blues vehicle, 'Hear My Train A-Comin'.

ROOM FULL OF MIRRORS

AT THE END of a lengthy April 1969 session at the Record Plant in New York, Hendrix, longtime friend Billy Cox and an unknown drummer cut this electrifying exercise in modernising the Delta blues. The last of 31 takes, this performance effectively buried the cryptic imagery of the song beneath a sonic barrage, led by some of Jimi's most ferocious guitar playing.

I DON'T LIVE TODAY

THE US-only *Lifelines* box set included a disc devoted to the Experience's concert at the Los Angeles Forum on April 26, 1969. After subduing the decidedly cantankerous audience, Hendrix blitzkrieged them with this frenetic revision of a song from his debut album.

LITTLE WING

HENDRIX was never more lyrical nor more sensitive than on this superb reading of 'Little Wing', taped at the Experience's February 24th 1969 Albert Hall show. Originally aired on the *Hendrix In The West* LP in the early Seventies, it remains one of his most magical live performances.

RED HOUSE/PURPLE HAZE

HENDRIX In The West also included another concert effort which was arguably definitive, via the version of 'Red House' taped in San Diego on May 25, 1969. For this box set, it was joined by a rendition of 'Purple Haze' from the same night, remixed since its first official exposure on the Stages set in 1992.

VOODOO CHILD (SLIGHT RETURN)

A THIRD revival from *Hendrix In The West*, this prematurely faded rendition of 'Voodoo Child' again came from the Albert Hall in February 1969.

IZABELLA

"I THINK I'm probably in the way", guitarist Larry Lee told bassist Billy Cox after their joint adventures – including the Woodstock festival – with Hendrix's summer-of-69 band, Gypsy, Sun & Rainbows. He was right, as proved by this first studio rendition of a song that remained in Jimi's repertoire for the next year. It only boasted a guide vocal, which was anything but passionate, but the cluttered landscape of this short-lived ensemble set the template for Hendrix's multi-dubbed experiments of the following year.

CD4

MESSAGE TO LOVE

B EGUN before the year-end Band Of Gypsys' gigs at the Fillmore East and completed afterwards, in January 1970, this studio rendition of the BOGs' anthem was deemed surplus to requirements after the trio's live album was prepared for release. In this form, it epitomised the qualities that aroused both love and loathing from different sets of fans: the rock-funk blend of Hendrix's guitar and the solid, immovable style of Buddy Miles' drumming.

EARTH BLUES

A NOTHER highlight of the BOG repertoire, this driving piece of rock'n'soul music was originally included on *Rainbow Bridge* in 1971, but only after Mitch Mitchell, who helped to assemble the album, had replaced Buddy Miles' drum track. History was reversed for this box set, allowing the track to be heard the way Hendrix might have intended – Ronettes' backing vocals and all.

ASTRO MAN

W HAT WAS little more than a private joke – as evidenced by the mock TV theme tune at the beginning – inspired Hendrix sufficiently for him to cut it twice, once with the Band Of Gypsys (the version heard here) and then later with Mitch Mitchell and Billy Cox (debuted on *The Cry Of Love*). In this form, it was funky, fun and eminently disposable.

COUNTRY BLUES

OPENING like the strange bastard child of 'Foxy Lady' and 'Star Spangled Banner' (Woodstock version), this Band Of Gypsys jam developed into a mildly unorthodox blues pattern, with an unidentified harmonica player wailing distantly off-mike. Country blues this wasn't, in any musicological sense, but it was quintessential Hendrix – just another musical excursion out of hundreds captured on tape, yet focused and inventive enough to deserve some kind of immortality.

FREEDOM

ONE OF THE most enlightening tracks on the entire box set, this February 1970 collaboration with Mitchell and Cox captured one of Hendrix's last great songs in the process of evolution. The intricate, almost Beatlesque guitar intro was rapidly discarded, as were many of the lyrics heard here, while the funky shuffle beat soon metamorphosed into something much more propulsive, both on stage and in later studio incarnations.

JOHNNY B. GOODE

MAINTAINING the secret agenda of reviving *Hendrix In The West* by stealth, the box set compilers retrieved this quite staggering piece of stagecraft, which stole Chuck Berry's rock'n'roll anthem from under its creator's nose. It was taped at Berkeley on May 30, 1970, and remains a potent example of Jimi's irrepressible genius as a guitar player.

LOVER MAN

IT WAS July 1970, and still Hendrix could not translate the almost guaranteed sparks produced by live renditions of the song into anything remotely as exciting in the studio. There were no obvious flaws in this Electric Lady Studios performance; but this was clearly one song which required an audience for it to shine.

BLUE SUEDE SHOES

THE FINAL contribution to this set from *Hendrix In The West* was also the least essential, by far: a soundcheck from Berkeley in May 1970, during which Hendrix, Cox and Mitchell subjected the mid-Fifties rock'n'roll anthem to ordeal by funk. The same performance was included on *Go Cat Go*, the final (1996) album by its original songwriter, Carl Perkins.

CHEROKEE MIST

BETWEEN June 1970 attempts at turning 'Astro Man' into something substantial, Hendrix, Mitchell and Cox explored this instrumental theme, previewing many of the patterns that would soon flourish under the title of 'In From The Storm'. The result was both skeletal and suitably misty, resembling a semi-familiar jam more than a structured composition.

COME DOWN HARD ON ME

DURING late 1969 and 1970, Hendrix slipped easily into half-formed funky blues excursions such as this one, which dated from mid-July 1970. Several takes emerged from that session, and a composite master was prepared by the engineers behind the *Loose Ends* compilation. The box set compilers opted for reportage rather than collage, by choosing one of the takes in its entirety.

HEY BABY/
IN FROM THE STORM

THE LO-FI and (so its makers claimed) 'official' release of the two so-called Rainbow Bridge concerts from Maui, Hawaii, on 30 July 1970 – see the Unofficial CDs section – couldn't come close to matching the sound quality of this genuinely official offering from the first of those shows. Heard here, this medley revealed the beauty of two

of Jimi's final songs, seamlessly merged in arguably the finest moment of the entire Maui experience.

EZY RYDER

SEVERAL Buddy Miles studio performances were replaced after Hendrix's death by Mitch Mitchell. Jimi favoured the opposite approach on this track, retaining only Miles' drum track from a Band Of Gypsys take and then overdubbing with the help of Traffic members Steve Winwood and Chris Wood, and twin vocalists the Ghetto Fighters. Like so much of his final year's studio work, the result was unsatisfyingly busy, verging on the over-anxious.

NIGHT BIRD FLYING

BEFORE the 'final' mix heard on *The Cry Of Love*, Hendrix had prepared this rough version of his tribute to DJ Alison Steele, which lacked his last set of guitar overdubs but compensated with recognisably different sonic effects.

ALL ALONG THE
WATCHTOWER/
IN FROM THE STORM

TWO POIGNANT moments from the Isle of Wight Festival, now released in full on *Blue Wild Angel*. 'Watchtower' came from early in the show, when Hendrix was battling valiantly against distortion and foreign sounds from his PA system; 'In From The Storm' was the last song of his final UK performance, delivered with chilling emotional directness.

SLOW BLUES

THE STORY ended here, with the final piece of multi-track tape Hendrix ever recorded – an otherwise inconsequential jam, given portentous significance by what happened next. The music stops in mid-note, eerily replicating the shocking suddenness of its creator's death the following month.

THE NEW HENDRIX CATALOGUE:

LIVE ALBUMS

BBC Sessions

MCA 11742 (UK), June 1998

BETWEEN JANUARY 30, AND DECEMBER 15, 1967, THE JIMI HENDRIX Experience recorded eight exclusive sessions for BBC Radio. Though these quickfire recordings represent a fascinating insight into the band's development that year, they weren't made for artistic or historic reasons. Instead, the Hendrix sessions, and thousands like them by artists major and minor, were required as an agreement with the Musicians' Union prevented the BBC from filling their shows with records: a certain percentage of the music which went out over the UK's airwaves had to be recorded specifically for the BBC, theoretically as live-in-the-studio performances (though the rules were bent to allow the minimum of overdubbing).

More than two decades after these tapes were made – and eighteen years after unofficial recordings of the shows began to circulate on bootlegs – the Hendrix Estate, via Alan Douglas, finally prepared a fully legal and (almost) accurately documented record of Jimi's encounters with the BBC. The result was 1989's *Radio One*, which thrilled consumers but dissatisfied completists by cherry-picking the 'best' (to Douglas' ears) of the Hendrix BBC archive.

Nine years later, with the Estate now in the hands of Experience Hendrix, collectors won out. *BBC Sessions* rounded up every track Jimi recorded for the Corporation – not just the full radio sessions, complete with out-takes, introductions and interviews, but also a pair of illuminating encounters with BBC TV. The limitations of the BBC studios in the Sixties ensured that this material could never rival the three-dimensional sonic glory of Hendrix's official output. But from its detailed annotation to its consistently enjoyable contents, *BBC Sessions* was a conceptual and creative triumph.

SESSION BY SESSION

Saturday Club

(recorded February 13, 1967)

TRACKS: Foxy Lady (2 takes)/Stone Free/Hey Joe (2 takes)/Love Or Confusion

SATURDAY CLUB WAS THE SHOWCASE OF THE BBC LIGHT PROGRAMME'S pop output: a weekly, two hour morning show hosted by the irrepressibly chirpy Brian Matthew. It rarely played host to anything other than live-in-the-studio facsimiles of recent records, and the Experience stayed true to the programme's spirit. What was most impressive, 30-plus years later, was the trio's ability to recreate the power of their studio releases, especially on the rarely performed 'Love Or Confusion'. The weaker of the two takes of 'Foxy Lady' and 'Hey Joe' weren't broadcast at the time, but BBC listeners were treated to a four-minute 'Hey Joe' that built on the skeleton of the hit single.

Saturday Club

(recorded March 28, 1967)

TRACKS: Fire/Purple Haze/Killing Floor

THE SURPRISINGLY SEDATE AND CERTAINLY PLAYFUL 'FIRE', AND ALMOST MANIC 'Killing Floor', were duly broadcast on *Saturday Club*, as intended. 'Purple Haze' was reserved for the BBC's Transcription Service, whereby overseas outlets were sent album-length discs entitled *Top Of The Pops*, which could be broadcast as complete radio shows.

Late Night Line Up

(recorded April 17, 1967)

TRACK: Manic Depression

MOST TV POP SHOWS IN 1967 REQUIRED BANDS TO MIME TO THEIR RECORDS, but for BBC-2's nightly arts show, the Experience performed live in front of the cameras as part of an experimental colour broadcast. Jimi's guitar was kept way too low in the mix, though that didn't prevent him from unleashing a wonderfully ambitious solo, and then chuckling to himself as he fumbled his riff in the following verse.

Top Gear

(recorded October 6, 1967)

TRACKS: Little Miss Lover/The Burning Of The Midnight Lamp/Catfish Blues/Hound Dog/Drivin' South (2 takes)/Jammin' (with Stevie Wonder)/I Was Made To Love Her (with Stevie Wonder)

AFTER THE BBC LIGHT PROGRAMME WAS DIVIDED INTO RADIO 1 (FOR POP FANS) and Radio 2 (for MOR music), *Top Gear* rapidly became the prime vehicle for exposing British listeners to underground rock. Brian Matthew used material from the Experience's memorable debut on the show for his *Top Of The Pops* Transcription programme (see above), including a rather sheepish group interview. The band reserved their confidence for the music, which ranged from a slightly erratic but still superb 'Midnight Lamp' to a hysterical romp through 'Hound Dog', complete with appropriate vocal effects. But the undoubted highlight was the broadcast version of the instrumental 'Drivin' South', a live favourite since Jimi's days with Curtis Knight. It was an astounding performance, swaggering and dramatic, and rarely equalled in the entire Experience catalogue.

BBC engineers also captured a few minutes of jamming between Hendrix, Noel Redding and the 17-year-old Stevie Wonder, another guest on the show. Wonder proved to be a slightly unreliable but wildly enthusiastic drummer, and once Hendrix had stopped worrying about the variable rhythm, he soared into an ecstatic guitar solo, presented here as 'Jammin'.

Alexis Korner's
Rhythm & Blues Show

(recorded October 17, 1967)

TRACKS: Can You Please Crawl Out Your Window/ I'm Your Hoochie Coochie Man *(sic)*/Drivin' South

KORNER, ONE OF THE PIONEERS OF BRITISH R&B, HOSTED THIS WEEKLY SHOW for listeners to the BBC World Service – which perhaps explained why Hendrix was happy to abandon his standard repertoire for the day. 'Can You Please Crawl Out Your Window' demonstrated his love for Bob Dylan, faithfully reproducing his hero's late 1965 single right down to the ad-libs. 'Drivin' South' ran longer than either of the Top Gear takes, and faded out before it finished, but couldn't match the intensity of the earlier renditions. But 'Hoochie Coochie Man' was more impressive, not least for the sonic contrast between Hendrix's nuclear-age lead, and the Chess-style slide guitar licks of Korner.

Top Gear

(recorded December 15, 1967)

TRACKS: Hear My Train A-Comin' (2 takes)/Radio One/Wait Until Tomorrow/ Day Tripper/Spanish Castle Magic

AS A FAREWELL TO BRITISH RADIO, THE EXPERIENCE DELIVERED THIS THOROUGHLY rowdy session, headed by perhaps the least emotionally intense version of 'Hear My Train A-Comin' that they ever performed. After transforming the blues into a party soundtrack, they romped through The Beatles' 'Day Tripper' (with Jimi alluding to another Fabs song, 'I Want To Tell You', as the tape started rolling) and a raucous 'Spanish Castle Magic'. The Experience even surprised the engineers by announcing that they'd prepared a jingle for the occasion: cue the raucous, but obviously rehearsed, 'Radio One'.

Note: Before its official release Redding's high harmonies on 'Day Tripper' convinced many an unwitting bootlegger that this track was some fabled jam between Jimi and John Lennon.

A Happening For Lulu

(recorded January 4, 1969)

TRACKS: Voodoo Child (Slight Return)/Hey Joe/Sunshine Of Your Love

THIS PROBABLY WASN'T THE KIND OF 'HAPPENING' THAT LULU WAS EXPECTING on her prime-time TV variety show. A slightly scrappy 'Voodoo Child' highlighted the gulf between the Experience and their audience, before Lulu encouraged the trio to revive 'Hey Joe' from two years earlier. It took Jimi almost a minute to stop playing free-form riffs and begin the song, and he quickly lost interest. With the TV producer gesticulating wildly from behind the cameras, the Experience careered into 'Sunshine Of Your Love' as a tribute to the recent dissembled Cream. Lulu's scripted farewell to the viewers was abandoned, as Hendrix and friends played right to the close of the credits – a rare piece of pre-punk anarchy in Britain's sedate TV schedule.

LIVE CONCERTS

Live At The Fillmore East

MCA 11931 (UK), February 1999

TRACKS

CD1: Stone Free/Power Of Soul/Hear My Train A-Comin'/ Izabella/Machine Gun/Voodoo Child (Slight Return)/We Gotta Live Together

CD2: Auld Lang Syne/Who Knows/Changes/Machine Gun/Stepping Stone/Stop/Earth Blues/Burning Desire/Wild Thing

IN JOHN MEDERMOTT'S STIRRING LINER NOTES, THE FOUR BAND OF GYPSYS concerts at the Fillmore East in New York represented "a critical turning point in a radiant career which boasted of infinite possibilities". And so they did, although not necessarily in a positive sense. The trio of Hendrix, Billy Cox and Buddy Miles carried enormous potential – check the Dagger CD *The Baggy's Rehearsal Sessions* for proof – but the Fillmore shows scarcely matched it.

Live At The Fillmore East was designed to demonstrate that the original *Band Of Gypsys* album didn't do justice to the grandeur and depth of those concerts. It boasted what might just have been the best-ever Hendrix album cover, and a track listing that promised to mix the cream of the BOGs' new songs with some adventurous return visits to Hendrix's back catalogue.

There were places where all the hype was fulfilled – notably, to no one's surprise, on the two additional performances of 'Machine Gun' included here. The take on the second CD, pulled from the late show on New Year's Eve 1969, was a real sonic adventure, while its companion on the first CD, taped the next day, took a markedly different approach to the same theme. Several of Jimi's extended solos were equally spectacular: 'Stone Free' found him building on the solid R&B groove of the band, while both 'Stepping Stone' (introduced here as 'Trying To Be') and 'Earth Blues' were rescued from unfocused playing by Hendrix's sheer determination to express himself.

But the rest was erratic, to say the least, with Buddy Miles' 'Changes' surviving the transition to the stage in healthier shape than 'Voodoo Child', 'Burning Desire' or the usually reliable 'Hear My Train A-Comin'. There were interesting diversions along the way: a big band version of 'Auld Lang Syne' giving way to the Gypsys' own interpretation, for instance, but that jam slipped into a stale march around the 'Who Knows' riff that outstayed its welcome in just four minutes.

Ultimately, there was little here to cause anyone to lament the early demise of the Band Of Gypsys. Buy *The Baggy's Rehearsal Sessions* instead, and hope that one day Experience Hendrix release all four takes of 'Machine Gun' from these gigs on a single disc.

Live At Woodstock

MCA 11987 (UK), July 1999

TRACKS
CD1: Introduction/Message To Love/Hear My Train A-Comin'/Spanish Castle Magic/Red House/Lover Man/Foxy Lady/Jam Back At The House
CD2: Izabella/Fire/Voodoo Child (Slight Return)/Star Spangled Banner/Purple Haze/Woodstock Improvisation/Villanova Junction/Hey Joe

I T HAS BECOME THE ULTIMATE SYMBOL OF THE SIXTIES: THREE DAYS OF LOVE, peace and music that united a generation. The reminiscences of those who attended the Woodstock Music and Art Fair in August 1969 are more ambivalent, however, as they remember the rain, the mud, the chaos, the traffic jams, the sanity-sapping brown acid. The *Woodstock* movie created a legend which has been ebbing slowly away ever since.

Certainly Jimi Hendrix would have shared the prevailing doubts about the Woodstock experience. He chose the occasion to unveil his experimental Gypsy, Sun & Rainbows Band, featuring two percussionists, another guitarist, plus Billy Cox and Mitch Mitchell. With this under-rehearsed ensemble, Jimi and his muse were sometimes able to wave affectionately at each other from passing trains, but they rarely locked onto the same track. There were moments when his fingers would flash fluently over the frets, only for the extended back-up crew to drag him back to mediocrity. As the exhausted crowd of half a million trickled away, there were thirty, maybe fifty thousand people there to witness artistry held in chains.

The true drama of his festival-closing performance came in its final 30 minutes. As a potentially brilliant 'Voodoo Child (Slight Return)' foundered into an appalling solo by second guitarist Larry Lee, and the band stumbled into an abortive 'Stepping Stone', Jimi realised that the battle was lost. "You can leave if you want to," he mumbled. "We're just jamming, that's all."

Then a stroke of electric genius: Jimi quietened the band, and entered the surreal territory of the 'Star Spangled Banner'. For the next four minutes, he and his guitar were united in an expression of flamboyant pain

– simultaneously exhibiting Hendrix's skills, and exorcising demons that could have been national or personal. Like the studio 'Voodoo Child (Slight Return)' or the Berkeley 'Johnny B. Goode', 'Star Spangled Banner' was a performance that made it impossible to separate the man from his music, as his guitar screeched through pained descents and exploded like fireworks over the exhausted remnants of the Woodstock crowd.

Suddenly triumphant, Jimi could crash through 'Purple Haze' without a moment's thought for finesse – then unwind into a thrilling guitar improvisation that wound in circles, teetering on the brink of incoherence, before easing effortlessly into the rehearsed patterns of the beautiful 'Villanova Junction', an exercise in structured melancholy. The finale of 'Hey Joe' was an anti-climax, but also a relief from the intense passion of what had gone before.

Almost all of the preamble to that remarkable climax was captured on the superbly packaged *Live At Woodstock*, though Experience Hendrix chose not to include the two songs that solely spotlighted Larry Lee, 'Mastermind' and 'Gypsy Woman', and did their best elsewhere to camouflage his out-of-tune playing.

Lee certainly sabotaged 'Lover Man' with a sloppy solo, while his rhythm chords added nothing to the standard trio vehicles of 'Hear My Train A-Comin'' or 'Red House'. They were among the highlights of the first hour of the performance, alongside Jimi's ferocious energy (though not the band's sluggishness) on 'Message To Love', and the rare sense of unity that Gypsy, Sun & Rainbows achieved on 'Spanish Castle Magic'. 'Jam Back At The House' and 'Izabella' also cohered, no doubt benefiting from pre-show rehearsals. But the rest was fascinating more for the contrast it presented with the triumphant finale than for its own musical merits.

Blue Wild Angel

MCA 113 086-2 (UK), November 2002

TRACKS
CD1: God Save The Queen/Sgt. Pepper's Lonely Hearts Club Band/Spanish Castle Magic/All Along The Watchtower/Machine Gun/Lover Man/Freedom/Red House/Dolly Dagger/Midnight Lightning
CD2: Foxy Lady/Message To Love/Hey Baby (New Rising Sun)/Ezy Ryder/Hey Joe/Purple Haze/Voodoo Child (Slight Return)/In From The Storm

Blue Wild Angel

(Highlights)

MCA 113 089-2 (UK), November 2002

TRACKS: God Save The Queen/Sgt. Pepper's Lonely Hearts Club Band/Spanish Castle Magic/All Along The Watchtower/Machine Gun/Lover Man/Freedom/Red House/Dolly Dagger/Hey Baby (New Rising Sun)/In From The Storm

THE *WOODSTOCK* MOVIE WAS RELEASED A COUPLE OF MONTHS BEFORE Jimi Hendrix appeared as the star attraction at the third Isle of Wight Festival – his last scheduled concert in Britain. *Woodstock*, with its carefully edited clip of Jimi's finest minutes at the 1969 festival, aroused impossible expectations of his UK visit, and the live set offered by Hendrix, Billy Cox and Mitch Mitchell rarely came close to meeting them.

As a psychodrama, the Isle of Wight show made for compelling viewing – Jimi never quite connected with the spiritual centre of his music, and his face reflected self-disgust allied with frustration as each attempt to bend the cacophonous noise of his guitar into structured sound collapsed into failure. Hendrix ended the show by tossing his instrument to the ground in a mixture of contempt and despair.

Even without the visuals, the elegantly packaged Blue Wild Angel captured both the anguish and the doomed courage of Hendrix's performance. With the exception of a handful of seconds lost when the 'Midnight Lightning' segue into 'Foxy Lady' was stupidly divided across the two CDs, it featured the entire Isle of Wight show, rendering both previous releases from this source – and the highlights package issued as a single CD – irrelevant.

The first half of the show was dogged by extraneous noise, with security guards, xylophones, static and even at one stage an opera singer audible above Hendrix and the band. The 22-minute 'Machine Gun' encapsulated the drama of the occasion, with Hendrix lost in a solitary world, desperately trying to play himself back into spirits, while constantly being jolted back to reality as another squeal or foreign sound burst from the speakers. After a floundering 'Lover Man', Jimi asked the audience to pretend he was starting over, and launched into a flawless rendition of 'Freedom' that could stand as a dictionary definition of liberation.

Yet still the battle between Hendrix and his devils wasn't over, and after an introspective, desperate 'Red House', he once again had to jam his way out of depression across the bluesy canvas of 'Midnight Lightning'. It was a brief moment of respite, before 'Foxy Lady' collapsed into a maelstrom of unrequested sound, and Hendrix stopped playing, leaving Mitchell and Cox to jam desultorily. "You all wanna hear those old songs, man? Damn", Jimi lamented, instead offering an erratic 'Message To Love'. And so the torture continued, before the audience recognised the familiar chords of 'Hey Joe', and Hendrix offered them the sop of a throwaway 'Purple Haze'.

'Voodoo Child (Slight Return)' took on the morbid tone of prophecy, as Jimi sang, "I ain't gonna see you no more in this world". Another song meandered to an inconclusive close, before Hendrix dug deep into his heart to produce an agonisingly naked 'In From The Storm', delivering the blues imagery with real despair. And then it was over. "Peace and happiness and all the other bullshit", he slurred, before the sound of his guitar hitting the stage signalled his departure. It was almost the end of an era, and a lifetime. Less than three weeks later, Hendrix was dead.

Live At Berkeley

MCA 0602498607527 (UK), October 2003

TRACKS: Introduction/Pass It On (Straight Ahead)/Hey Baby (New Rising Sun)/Lover Man/Stone Free/Hey Joe/I Don't Live Today/Machine Gun/Foxy Lady/Star Spangled Banner/Purple Haze/Voodoo Child (Slight Return)

IT'S UNCLEAR WHY EXPERIENCE HENDRIX OPTED TO CONCENTRATE ON THE SECOND of the two remarkable shows that Jimi performed at the Berkeley Community Theatre on May 30, 1970. A double-CD of both sets might have comprised a real landmark in the Hendrix catalogue. Not that the presentation of *Live At Berkeley* was in any way below par, though. The album captured Messrs Hendrix, Cox and Mitchell in front of a wildly responsive crowd, opening proceedings with a set of new material.

The rudimentary lyrics of 'Pass It On' (an early version of 'Straight Ahead') perfectly caught the political tension of the era – and the evening, with riot police having to break up disappointed fans. But the delicacy of 'Hey Baby' (which the crowd greeted with approval, assuming that Hendrix was beginning 'Hey Joe') balanced the mood. Propulsive versions of 'Lover Man' and 'Stone Free' followed, before 'Hey Joe' appeared in the flesh – accompanied by unwanted chatter and feedback through the amps that simply heightened the eerie atmosphere of the performance. 'I Don't Live Today' was delivered with savage energy, but 'Machine Gun' demonstrated the range of Hendrix's emotional responses this evening, by accentuating lyricism instead of the anger heard during the Band Of Gypsys renditions of the song.

Aside from a rather perfunctory 'Star Spangled Banner', lacking any of the depth of the Woodstock performance, the remainder of the set was feisty and alive. 'Voodoo Child' drifted into a 'Keep On Groovin' jam, with the three musicians demonstrating a mutual awareness sadly lacking on their next official live release, at the Isle of Wight three months later.

THE HERITAGE:

STUDIO ALBUMS

The Cry Of Love

LP release: Track 2408 101 (UK), March 1971
CD release: Polydor 829 926-2 (UK), March 1989
CD reissued on Polydor 847 242-2 (UK), March 1993

TRACKS: Freedom/Drifting/Ezy Ryder/Night Bird Flying/My Friend/Straight
Ahead/Astro Man/Angel/In From The Storm/Belly Button Window

IT WAS PRESENTED FIVE MONTHS AFTER HIS DEATH AS JIMI'S FINAL ALBUM, as though there had never been any debate about its contents. But drummer Mitch Mitchell (who added some subtle overdubs to various tracks) and engineer Eddie Kramer, the co-compilers of *The Cry Of Love*, were working to a plan of their own design. They chose to ignore both the title and the planned format (a double-LP set, remember) of *The First Rays Of The New Rising Sun*. They also omitted the effectual title track of Jimi's grandiose project, 'Hey Baby (The Land Of The New Rising Sun)', plus songs like 'Dolly Dagger' (introduced by Hendrix at the Isle of Wight as "a song we're trying to get together for our next album"), 'Midnight Lightning' and 'Room Full Of Mirrors', all of which Mitch had been playing on stage with Jimi in the months leading up to his death.

In many ways, the second posthumous album, the pretend soundtrack LP *Rainbow Bridge*, actually came closer to realising Hendrix's dream of *New Rising Sun* than did *The Cry Of Love*. But it's likely that Mitch and Eddie's sole aim was to produce a commercial album as quickly as possible, to satisfy the demands of both Jimi's audience and his record company – who were no doubt relieved that the double-LP had been chopped down to a single record.

For all that, *The Cry Of Love* (the name Jimi gave his band on his spring 1970 US tour) was a disappointingly subdued affair – more inspired than *Band Of Gypsys*, it's true, but scarcely on a level with the sonic and artistic invention of *Electric Ladyland*. It added weight to those who suggested that Hendrix had run into some kind of musical block in the months leading up to his death.

As it was not regarded as an 'official' Hendrix album, *The Cry Of Love* never underwent the full remastering process awarded to Jimi's

Electric Gypsy. Jimi backstage at *Top Of The Pops*, May 1967.
(Harry Goodwin)

The Nineties CD inlay that reproduces the classic UK album sleeve for Jimi's debut album *Are You Experienced* (1967).

The Jimi Hendrix Experience, Germany, March 1967 - L-R: Noel Redding, Jimi, Mitch Mitchell. *(Gunter Zint/Redferns)*

The US version of *Are You Experienced* (1967).

Miming 'Hey Joe' on *Top Of The Pops*, January 1967. *(LFI)*

Jimi in rehearsal, 1967. *(LFI)*

The sleeve to *Axis: Bold As Love*, the second Experience album, 1967.

Beat Club TV broadcast taped at London's Marquee Club, 2nd March 1967. *(Marc Sharratt/Rex Features)*

A rare moment to relax off stage, 1967. *(LFI)*

A bag full of tricks. Jimi plays behind his head,
UK Walker Brothers package tour, March 1967 *(LFI)*

The 'Experienced' trio backstage, 1967. *(LFI)*

The Nineties CD inlay that reproduces the classic UK album sleeve for Jimi's third (and double) album *Electric Ladyland* (1968).

The sanitised US cover for *Electric Ladyland*.

Jimi poses in Montagu Place, London. At the time he was living in nearby Montagu Square. *(Magnus/Rex Features)*

Jimi with original mentor/producer Chas Chandler. The two parted company due to the unproductive carousing during the *Electric Ladyland* sessions. (LFI)

Jimi ended 1967 as fully established in Europe and
a top draw in his native America. *(LFI)*

earlier records.

There were two UK versions of the disc, both with a minimalist booklet that credited 'Jimmi Hendrix' as co-producer, and had him writing "helly my friend" in the liner-note poem. The earlier CD transfer succeeded in clipping off the first chord of 'Freedom'; the second edition wasn't perfect, by any means, but did offer clearer and louder sound. Both editions were superseded in 1997 when the entire album was included on *First Rays Of The New Rising Sun* in vastly superior mixes.

Rainbow Bridge

LP release: Reprise K 41459 (UK), November 1971
CD release: Reprise K 2231459 (Japan), March 1987

TRACKS: Dolly Dagger/Earth Blues/Pali Gap/Room Full Of Mirrors/Star Spangled Banner/Look Over Yonder/Hear My Train A-Comin'/Hey Baby (New Rising Sun)

WHY WAS *RAINBOW BRIDGE* SO MUCH MORE IMPRESSIVE THAN *THE CRY OF Love*? Why did it purport to be a film soundtrack album, when it only had a few minutes of music from the film? And why was it never released on CD in Britain or America?

The spur for this release was the *Rainbow Bridge* film, which tacked around 20 minutes of a Hendrix live performance from on top of a Hawaiian volcano (actually known as Rainbow Ridge) with more than an hour of tortuous, inane hippie psycho-babble. No-one who'd watched the movie on anything less mind-altering than acid would have considered buying the album for a second.

The entire deal was manager Mike Jeffery's way of establishing his counter-culture credentials, by letting film-maker Chuck Wein inveigle Jimi and band into his ridiculous movie. Jeffery agreed to furnish Warner Brothers Films with a soundtrack album, only to discover after Jimi's death that the Hawaii performance hadn't been adequately recorded. (As an example, Mitch Mitchell had to re-dub all his drum parts for the movie, the original track being unusable.)

With the assistance of Eddie Kramer, Mike Jeffery finally assembled an album that dragged every possible contender from a variety of tape sources – several of the songs having been pulled from the pool of material Jimi had been stockpiling for *The First Rays Of The New Rising Sun*. But although this haphazard approach was far from foolproof, it did unearth some recordings that evoked Jimi's dream of a rock/soul crossover far more successfully than the rather laboured *The Cry Of Love*.

The oldest song on the album was 'Look Over Yonder' (alias 'Mr. Bad Luck', under which title Jimi had been performing it since the pre-Experience days of 1966). He'd cut a studio version with Noel Redding and Mitch Mitchell in May 1967, but the R&B-flavoured *Rainbow Bridge* take hailed from the post-*Electric Ladyland* sessions of October 1968. 'Star Spangled Banner' aroused great expectations from those who'd seen the *Woodstock* movie, but the March 1969 studio take was an abomination alongside that epochal rendition. Cloaked in double-speed guitar overdubs, it was passionless, synthesised and almost unlistenable.

Everything else on the album came from the last year of Hendrix's life. 'Earth Blues' (with The Ronettes, no less, on backing vocals) and 'Room Full Of Mirrors' were cut during the abortive Band Of Gypsys studio sessions around Christmas 1969, and perfectly illustrated the modest ambitions of the Hendrix/Miles/Cox line-up. Three further songs were pulled from July 1970 sessions featuring Cox and Mitchell, including the virtual title song of the album Jimi was trying to complete when he died, 'Hey Baby (New Rising Sun)', the sparkling 'Dolly Dagger', a riff-rocker dedicated to girlfriend Devon Wilson, and the instrumental 'Pali Gap' – named by Mike Jeffery in a vain attempt to give the LP some Hawaiian ambience.

Ironically, the finest performance on *Rainbow Bridge* wasn't a studio cut at all, but a song from the Berkeley shows in May 1970 that would also supply some stellar moments to the next album, *Hendrix In The West*. 'Hear My Train A-Comin'' supplanted 'Red House' as Jimi's ultimate expression of the blues in his final year, and this is undoubtedly the definitive rendition – a ten-minute exercise in "less is more", in direct contrast to the over-egged trickery of 'Star Spangled Banner'. For this track alone, *Rainbow Bridge* has to be heard.

Unlike the rest of the original Seventies posthumous albums, *Rainbow Bridge* was only issued on CD in Japan – and even then it was only available for a few months. "I have my problems with *Rainbow Bridge* as an album," Alan Douglas explained in 1990. "It's not a real soundtrack; those were just studio tapes that his management put together to make a record." Four years later, he added: "*Rainbow Bridge* has a lot of filler in it." That was a dubious proposition, at best, but the entire contents of the original LP were eventually issued on CD, divided between *The First Rays Of The New Rising Sun*, *South Saturn Delta*, *Blues* and *Jimi Hendrix Experience*.

War Heroes

LP release: Polydor 2302 020 (UK), October 1972
CD release: Polydor 813 573-2 (UK), March 1989

TRACKS: Bleeding Heart/Highway Chile/Tax Free/Peter Gunn Catastrophe/ Stepping Stone/Midnight/Three Little Bears/Beginning/Izabella

THE TITLE OF THIS RAGBAG OF HENDRIX LEFTOVERS OWED MORE TO THE DATE of its release, at the height of anti-Vietnam feeling in America, than any relevance to its contents. With the aid of engineer Eddie Kramer, Mike Jeffery assembled what was promoted as the first album of Jimi's out-takes, rather than the supposedly complete tracks that were included on *The Cry Of Love* and *Rainbow Bridge*. Three tracks, at least, had been approved by Hendrix: 'Highway Chile' was the flipside of 'The Wind Cries Mary', while 'Stepping Stone'/'Izabella' was a Band Of Gypsys single, admittedly pulled from the shops within days of its release. Both those rock/funk crossovers were remixed for *War Heroes*, while Mitch Mitchell replaced Buddy Miles' piledriving drum part on 'Stepping Stone'.

For the rest of the album, the compilers had to wade through a variety of session tapes, covering more than two years. There were two out-takes from *Electric Ladyland*: the instrumental 'Tax Free' (written by the Swedish duo Hansson & Karlsson, who taught it to Jimi during an after-hours Stockholm jam in September 1967); and the cod reggae tune 'Three Little Bears', on which Jimi delivered his own verdict early in the proceedings: "I don't know if I can go through with this, it's really silly."

Noel Redding's 'Midnight', an instrumental riff in 'Foxy Lady' vein, came from the Experience's last batch of sessions in April 1969, while Elmore James' 'Bleeding Heart' was another Band Of Gypsys outing – again with Mitchell's overdubs. Hendrix had been performing the song since at least 1965, and an earlier studio cut was included on the *Blues* CD in 1994. The remaining tracks dated from the summer of 1970: 'Beginning', better known from its Woodstock appearance as 'Jam Back At The House', was a Mitch Mitchell composition, though Hendrix virtually claimed it as his own with an intense solo; while the aptly named 'Peter Gunn Catastrophe' saw Hendrix, Mitchell and Billy Cox cruising through Henry Mancini's *Peter Gunn* TV theme, before collapsing into a parody of the Frankie Laine hit 'Jealousy'. With this track (which has never been reissued) and 'Three Little Bears' on board, the good ship *War Heroes* was sailing through treacherous waters – and the worldwide sales of the album were disappointing.

Packaged on CD with the bare minimum of (often erroneous) information, *War Heroes* was a disgrace. 'Bleeding Heart' and 'Midnight' were wrongly credited as Hendrix songs; and there were no musician credits or recording dates. The disc listed different titles for two songs to those on the back cover. Worst of all, the spine of the CD credited someone called 'Jimmi Hendrix'.

Loose Ends

LP release: Polydor 2310 301 (UK), February 1974
CD release: Polydor 837 574-2 (UK), March 1989

TRACKS: Coming Down Hard On Me Baby/Blue Suede Shoes/Jam 292/ The Stars That Play With Laughing Sam's Dice/Drifter's Escape/Burning Desire/I'm Your Hoochie Coochie Man *(sic)*/Electric Ladyland

AT LEAST THE TITLE WAS HONEST. EDDIE KRAMER DIDN'T WANT ANY MORE PART in the discrediting of Hendrix's reputation: his assistant engineer, John Jansen, told author John McDermott: "Mike Jeffery kept pressing for 'just one more'. Anything that remotely sounded like music was worth going to Polydor and getting money for an album."

In his book, *Setting The Record Straight*, McDermott described *Loose Ends* as "a callous and shameful exercise". He was not wrong. It was undoubtedly the worst album ever officially approved by the various curators of the Hendrix legacy, and it's impossible to imagine that Jimi would have wanted the public to hear a single second of it.

The one exception to that rule was the one track that Jimi himself released, the 1967 B-side 'The Stars That Play With Laughing Sam's Dice' – a mind-altering journey in concept and sound. Only one other song on *Loose Ends* deserved that acclaim – the solo rendition of 'Electric Ladyland'. Its 92 seconds of beauty followed more than 15 minutes of Band Of Gypsys jamming, as Hendrix, Miles and Cox worked through the twists and turns of 'Burning Desire' and made heavy weight of 'Hoochie Coochie Man'.

Even less appealing was 'Blue Suede Shoes', a four-minute Band Of Gypsys track which comprised less than two minutes of song and far too much studio badinage. If you needed to hear Jimi joking around with 'Heartbreak Hotel', this is where you came. Just be grateful that Jeffery didn't insist on the inclusion of the full 11-minute jam from which this sorry track was pulled.

Hendrix's arrangements of Bob Dylan's 'Like A Rolling Stone' (at Monterey) and 'All Along The Watchtower' (on *Electric Ladyland*) might whet the appetite for another Dylan cover, 'Drifter's Escape'. But this May 1970 recording, one of the first at Jimi's own Electric Lady Studios, smothered the song in musical clutter, subduing its original acoustic rhythms beneath the chatter of funk guitars. Two months later, the same musicians rambled through the blues-soul of 'Coming Down Hard On Me Baby', an undeveloped and certainly not complete song in the making.

By far the least enticing title on *Loose Ends* was 'Jam 292', named by Jeffery after its studio tape number. Ironically, though, this impromptu mix of blues structure and wah-wah guitar, with Hendrix accompanied by Stephen Stills and drummer Dallas Taylor, was one of the album's most impressive tracks. It was still little more than inconsequential, however, which is an apt summary of the entire record.

Given only the most cursory of CD remastering jobs, *Loose Ends* also suffered from appalling cover design, erroneous credits (no mention of Stills and Taylor, for instance, and 'Hoochie Coochie Man' given the wrong composer and title) and a complete lack of annotation.

Crash Landing

LP release: Polydor 2310 398 (UK), August 1975
CD release: Polydor 827 932-2 (UK), March 1989

TRACKS: Message To Love/Somewhere Over The Rainbow/Crash Landing/ Coming Down Hard On Me Baby/Peace In Mississippi/With The Power/ Stone Free/Captain Coconut

JIMI HENDRIX FIRST APPROACHED ALAN DOUGLAS, ENTREPRENEUR AND JAZZ label boss, in September 1969. Douglas attended one of Jimi's most chaotic studio sessions, after which the guitarist told him that he needed help to supervise his projects, and prevent his recording attempts from being overrun by well-wishers, hangers-on and more nefarious characters.

Douglas and Hendrix remained in some kind of contact for the remaining year of Jimi's life, but Alan was sidelined by Mike Jeffery's dominance over the first three years of posthumous releases. Jeffery's death in a March 1973 plane crash, in circumstances that many regarded as sinister, opened the gates for new curators to take control of Jimi's artistic legacy. Douglas had financed the recording of several Hendrix jams, and as the owner of unissued material he was approached by Warner Brothers after Jeffery's demise in the hope that he could provide the label with something that could be salvaged for commercial release. Given this window of opportunity, Douglas began to investigate other possible tape sources and unearthed a quantity of unfinished recordings made at the Record Plant in New York, which he reckoned were possible contenders for release.

According to John McDermott, Douglas laid out the running order for an album he titled *Crash Landing*, which would feature: 'Crash Landing', 'Somewhere', 'With The Power', 'New Rising Sun', 'Message To Love', an untitled jam, 'Stone Free', 'Peace In Mississippi' and 'Here Comes Your Lover Man'. Listening back to the tapes, though, Douglas realised that the ensemble playing of the Band Of Gypsys, the Experience and the Cry Of Love band was too shambolic for release in its current state.

So he took the tapes, and the problem, to top studio engineer Tony Bongiovi. The two men agreed on a solution, albeit an endlessly controversial one: the original tapes should not only be remixed but also overdubbed by session musicians, to approximate the musical vision inherent but dormant within the existing tracks.

In many cases, Bongiovi and Douglas were working on material already rejected by Eddie Kramer and John Jansen. But the latter pair had started from the idea that they would simply be transferring the best of Hendrix's work from master-tape to record. The new régime had more ambitious and creative work in mind.

Their involvement was certainly painstaking. This was no haphazard overdubbing of impromptu bass and drum parts. Instead, Bongiovi assembled every possible take of each song, and reviewed their potential for cannibalising. Guitar solos were extracted from a take which had an unsatisfactory rhythm track, and married to the bass and drums from another. Thereafter, the session musicians – chosen in preference to Jimi's original sidemen because they needed to be fluent sight-readers, working from transcriptions of the original performances – filled in the gaps, bar by arduous bar.

Purists have decried the results ever since: almost all of *Crash Landing* was music that Jimi Hendrix never heard, at least in that form. The decision not to use Jimi's own choice of musicians to complete the recordings was universally criticised, though Douglas's excuse – that Mitch Mitchell or Billy Cox wouldn't have been experienced enough as studio players to repair odd bars or half-bars of missing music – wasn't covered in the press at the time.

Was the album an abomination, then, from start to finish? Far from it. On purely aural evidence (i.e. without voicing an opinion on the morals of the exercise), *Crash Landing* was a fine record, probably more enjoyable to hear than any of the posthumous studio releases apart from *Rainbow Bridge*. The earliest original recording on the album was 'Somewhere Over The Rainbow', which had featured the rare combination of Buddy Miles and Noel Redding back in March 1968. Their efforts were wiped and replaced, leaving Hendrix's echoed vocals surrounded by layers of guitar as he imagined the reactions of aliens looking at the planet from their swooping UFOs. The Experience recording of 'Peace In Mississippi' from October 1968 was almost completely obliterated during the concoction of *Crash Landing*; even one of Jimi's rhythm guitar tracks was erased. The result was a scorching blues instrumental on which it was difficult to distinguish what was Hendrix and what was session guitarist Jeff Mironov.

The album's title track, a scathing dissection of a failing romance that incorporated some intriguing lyrics about drug use, and a vocal riff borrowed from The Beatles' 'Happiness Is A Warm Gun', was as impressive as anything on the record. It was originally taped in April 1969, as was 'Stone Free Again', a revamp of the 1966 B-side. Jimi's vocal on the *Crash Landing* reconstruction was compressed and thinned as if it had been recorded down a phone line.

'Message To Love' and 'With The Power' (alias 'Power Of Soul') had both been included on the *Band Of Gypsys* album back in 1970. The studio versions received far less tinkering than anything else on the LP, and stood for many years as perhaps the most impressive Gypsys' cuts available on record. In particular, 'Message To Love' – distressingly laboured on *Band Of Gypsys* – finally hit Jimi's conception of a soul/rock crossover head on.

'Coming Down Hard On Me Baby', aired a year earlier on *Loose Ends*, didn't deserve its *Crash Landing* revamp. But the final track, named 'Captain Coconut' by Alan Douglas, was a more intriguing affair – an electronic composition, no less, for electric guitar, slipping delicately through moods and movements in an almost classical vein. 'Captain Coconut' was not a track that Hendrix would have recognised. Based on material from tape boxes marked 'MLK' (claimed by some commentators to refer to civil rights leader Martin Luther King), it had actually been assembled from three separate groups of sessions by John Jansen, when he was creating incidental Hendrix music for the *Rainbow Bridge* movie. Eddie Kramer objected to Jansen tampering with unconnected Hendrix fragments, but Douglas and Bongiovi accepted the piece on its undoubted musical merits, and overdubbed it accordingly. So was 'Captain Coconut' a minor Hendrix masterpiece, a perversion of the truth, or both? Your reaction to that question is likely to determine your opinion of the entire *Crash Landing* project.

The album might have enjoyed a better critical reception if its origins and preparation had been explained in some detailed sleeve-notes. Instead, the LP – and its CD transfer – simply listed the musicians on each cut, with no indication of whether their contributions were made in 1968 or 1975. Worse still, Alan Douglas awarded himself a co-writing credit for five tracks: 'Somewhere Over The Rainbow', 'Crash Landing', 'Coming Down Hard On Me Baby', 'Peace In Mississippi' and 'Captain Coconut'.

Midnight Lightning

LP release: Polydor 2310 415 (UK), November 1975
CD release: Polydor 825 166-2 (UK), March 1989

TRACKS: Trashman/Midnight Lightning/Hear My Train A-Coming *(sic)*/Gypsy Boy (New Rising Sun)/Blue Suede Shoes/Machine Gun/Once I Had A Woman/Beginnings

LIKE *CRASH LANDING*, *MIDNIGHT LIGHTNING* WAS ASSEMBLED BY ALAN DOUGLAS and Tony Bongiovi. Interviewed 15 years later by *Guitar Player* magazine, Douglas admitted that the second recycling exercise had been a failure:"We were light on material, and I think I forced the issue in a couple of instances. It's just not thoroughly enjoyable, and it's not the best of Hendrix."

That was certainly true of 'Blue Suede Shoes', which was a travesty on *Loose Ends* and wasn't rescued by the Douglas-supervised overdubs. Nor was the stripping away of Mitch Mitchell and Noel Redding's contributions to Noel's 'Midnight' (first released on *War Heroes*) a success – especially when the track was re-titled 'Trashman', with the composer credit switching from Redding to Hendrix.

Equally insensitive was the decision to work on another *War Heroes* track, Mitch Mitchell's 'Beginning', and to wipe its writer's drum track from the tape. At least in the case of the clichéd blues jam, 'Once I Had A Woman' (given its title by Douglas), the raw material wasn't much to begin with.

Those disasters accounted for half of *Midnight Lightning*, but the remaining four tracks were all regular inclusions in Jimi's 1969/1970 live sets. 'Machine Gun' was the stand-out cut on *Band Of Gypsys*, for instance, but this studio rehash managed to undercut any of the song's aural drama, blurring the essence of Hendrix's anti-war lament (and a wonderful guitar solo) beneath an amateurish mix and some ill-considered session playing.

Equally ill-fated was 'Hear My Train A-Coming' *(sic)* (alias 'Getting My Heart Back Together Again'), usually a vehicle for some of Jimi's most passionate blues playing, and 'Gypsy Boy', a re-titling of 'Hey Baby (New Rising Sun)' which bore none of the precision of the *Rainbow Bridge* original. Finally, the album's title track epitomised the nature of the album: a pleasant, if inconsequential blues performance buried beneath excess instrumentation and gospel vocals. Was this a clue to the way Hendrix's music would have developed, or an abomination? Most fans veered towards the latter view.

Nine To The Universe

LP release: Polydor 2344 155 (UK), June 1980
Unreleased on official CD

TRACKS: Nine To The Universe/Jimi-Jimmy Jam/Young-Hendrix/Easy Blues/Drone Blues

THE THIRD AND (FOR THE MOMENT) LAST OF ALAN DOUGLAS'S 'CREATIONS' FROM the unissued Hendrix archives attracted a much lower profile than *Crash Landing* or *Midnight Lightning*, with sales to match. Hendrix was scarcely a commercial force in 1980: issued five years earlier, or ten later, *Nine To The Universe* might have been greeted as some kind of event.

For years, Douglas had been touting the musical genius of an impromptu jam session between Hendrix and jazz-rock guitarist John McLaughlin. *Nine To The Universe* seemed like the ideal venue for this tape, but McLaughlin himself expressed his dissatisfaction with the standard of his playing, and presumably blocked the release of the album Douglas had originally intended.

Instead, the LP borrowed from a variety of Hendrix jam sessions, which to varying degrees supported Douglas' claim that Jimi was moving towards jazz in his final years. More accurate would be the acknowledgement that Hendrix loved to jam: there are countless post-1967 tapes, both live and studio, to prove it.

With the exception of the piece that gave this album its name, none of the tracks were 'songs' as such: they were selected, edited and then titled by Alan Douglas, not Hendrix. Longer versions of all five exist on bootleg tapes, incidentally. 'Jimi/Jimmy Jam' matched Hendrix with guitarist Jim McCarty (not the Yardbirds drummer but a member of the Buddy Miles Express). It was taped on March 25, 1969; almost a month later, on April 24, Jimi and some unidentified musicians recorded the aptly titled 'Drone Blues', marked by some astounding Hendrix guitar passages.

May 14, 1969 produced the most fruitful of these jams, 'Young/Hendrix', on which Jimi was joined by Billy Cox, Buddy Miles and renowned avant-jazz organist Larry Young. For almost the only time on the record, 'Young/Hendrix' confirmed the claims of those who regard Hendrix as a pure jazz genius in the making. Eight days later, Hendrix, Cox and Miles were back in the Record Plant studios cutting 'Message From Nine To The Universe' – in which could clearly be heard the seeds for two songs the trio would play later in the year as the Band Of Gypsys: 'Message To Love' and 'Earth Blues'. Finally, 'Easy Blues' captured the core of the band that played at Woodstock – Jimi, Larry Lee, Mitch, Juma and Billy – swinging with a lack of inhibition that would have been more usefully displayed at the festival.

Nine To The Universe would make a wonderful bootleg – in fact, in the absence of an official CD, it duly became one, complete with bonus tracks – but it was scarcely a commercial proposition, or a valid attempt to portray Hendrix as a potential jazzman. But it did attract far more favourable reviews than either of Douglas' posthumous studio concoctions of the mid-Seventies.

Jimi By Himself: The Home Recordings

Penguin BSP-VC 1 (US), 1995

TRACKS: 1983 … (A Merman I Should Turn To Be)/Angel/Cherokee Jam/Hear My Train A-Comin'/Voodoo Chile-Cherokee Mist (medley)/Gypsy Eyes

THIS AUDIO VERITÉ SET OF DEMOS, RECORDED IN JIMI'S MANHATTAN APARTMENT in spring 1968, first surfaced on such bootlegs as *Acoustic Jam* (though they were actually performed on lightly amplified electric guitar). In 1995, thanks to the generosity of Alan Douglas, they were included in far superior sound quality as a bonus disc tucked inside the back cover of a graphic novel based on Hendrix's life. *Voodoo Child: The Illustrated Legend Of Jimi Hendrix* was created and produced by Martin I. Green, illustrated by Bill Sienkiewicz, and was well regarded by those who liked that kind of thing. But for many collectors, the 26-minute CD was a more compelling reason to buy.

Intimate and revelatory, it featured Jimi previewing and experimenting with some of the material he had assembled for *Electric Ladyland*. Aside from 'Angel', instantly recognisable in this stripped down form, and the fragment of 'Hear My Train A-Comin'', the other songs bore little resemblance to their later studio incarnations. '1983' was an obvious highlight, packing an emotional punch even without the sonic tapestry of the studio behind it. But 'Gypsy Eyes' was scarcely recognisable beyond the chorus motif, while the 'Voodoo Chile' improvisation kept threatening to break into 'If Six Was Nine' in its search for a route through the Delta blues. The entire tape deserves a wider hearing on a future release.

Voodoo Soup

Polydor 527 520-2 (UK), April 1995

TRACKS: The New Rising Sun/Belly Button Window/Stepping Stone/ Freedom/Angel/Room Full Of Mirrors/Midnight/Night Bird Flying/ Drifting/Ezy Ryder/Pali Gap/Message To Love/Peace In Mississippi/In From The Storm

A T THE START OF 1994, ALAN DOUGLAS REVEALED TO *ICE* MAGAZINE THAT HE was on the verge of solving the dilemma of how to present the unfinished studio project that was cut short by Jimi's death. He announced that he was planning a release entitled *First Rays Of The New Rising Sun*: "I have Jimi's track listing for it, and originally I was going to release the album just the way he wrote it out. But as I look at it, I'm sure he would have changed it fourteen times before it was released. So I'm going to do a little contest among the fans, saying, 'Give me 78 minutes of *First Rays*'."

A year later, Douglas was back on the phone to *ICE*: "I don't believe I can fulfill Jimi's concept of *First Rays* with the material that we have, because, frankly, he couldn't. The songs come from two years of no continuity. He had four bands in those years, at ten different studios. He changed the name of the album a thousand times. He was just focusing on songs, and trying to work in between problems with his management, and the group breaking up."

It was an honest assessment of a difficult period, but also preparation for a bold – some said foolhardy – Douglas coup. Instead of the definitive *First Rays*, he released *Voodoo Soup*: a self-parodying title, perhaps, for a collection of studio out-takes from a variety of sources, linked by the fact that they post-dated the completion of *Electric Ladyland*. It was, Douglas said, "Jimi jumping in and out of the kitchen, throwing some tracks in and mixing the soup up".

Not that Douglas was averse to his own mixing – or altering. Two decades after he'd scandalised fans by adding new overdubs to Hendrix recordings, he was at it again, with former Knack drummer Bruce Gary replacing Buddy Miles' original percussion on 'Stepping Stone' and 'Room Full Of Mirrors'. This move aroused fury amongst Hendrix aficionados, and the controversy overshadowed the fact that – this tinkering aside – *Voodoo Soup* was actually a superbly programmed and eminently listenable collection that served Jimi's memory well.

Like Eddie Kramer and the rest of the Experience Hendrix team, Douglas's first aim was to make Hendrix sound alive to new generations of listeners. To this end, his team (subtly and otherwise) remixed and revamped many familiar recordings from the albums issued immediately after Jimi's death. On 'Freedom', for example, they reversed the left/right channels for the two main guitar parts, and deleted the third, rather intrusive overdub heard on *The Cry Of Love*. 'Night Bird Flying' benefited from a more organic mix than on the original 1970 LP. Elsewhere, on 'Drifting' and 'Stepping Stone', previously buried guitar parts were uncovered.

Three tracks were added to the Hendrix canon. 'Belly Button Window' was an alternate take to the one found on *The Cry Of Love*. 'Peace In Mississippi' was exhumed from an October 1968 tape reel, having been subjected to some of Douglas' most hamfisted overdubs on *Crash Landing* 20 years earlier. Finally, the opening track, 'New Rising Sun', was rescued from its previous fate as one of the constituent parts of the posthumously assembled 'Captain Coconut'. Returned to the form in which Hendrix had left it, it was revealed as a subtle overture of guitar overdubs – and a poignant introduction to an album that belonged in every collection of the man's work.

Morning Symphony Ideas

Dagger 088-112-353-2 (US), July 2000

TRACKS: Keep On Groovin'/Jungle/Room Full Of Mirrors/Strato Strut/Scorpio Woman/Acoustic Demo

BOOTLEGGERS HAVE LONG SINCE RAIDED THE APPARENTLY ENDLESS ARCHIVE of Hendrix jam sessions and home recordings, and the launch of Dagger Records gave the Experience Hendrix crew the opportunity to market similar material themselves without needing to target a mass audience.

Despite its grandiose title, the contents of *Morning Symphony Ideas* were improvisational rather than conceptual in nature. Almost 50 minutes of material documented the Band Of Gypsys at the Record Plant in New York – with all but one track featuring simply Hendrix and Buddy Miles. 'Room Full Of Mirrors' was taped at the September 1969 session when Miles replaced Mitch Mitchell in the band, so it necessarily found Hendrix leading the way, and the drummer responding vivaciously to the unfamiliar changes. The recording cut off just as Jimi was about to launch into 'Machine Gun', which would become the BOGs' live anthem.

Seven weeks later, Hendrix and Miles romped through a 28-minute jam dubbed 'Keep On Groovin' on this set. Along the way, they touched on several staples of the band's repertoire – 'Power Of Soul', 'Burning Desire', 'Stepping Stone' – and through it all Hendrix reeled off a diverse set of preplanned riffs and patterns. But it was jamming, not genius, and one hearing will satisfy most listeners. The same applied to 'Jungle', which opened with a Curtis Mayfield feel, rich with grace notes and flickers of melody, before drifting into a mix of familiar BOGs-era riffs.

In December 1969, meanwhile, Billy Cox was finally on hand for 'Strato Strut', a jam neatly described by its title. Chronologically, what came next was 'Acoustic Demo' – a generous title for 68 seconds of blues riffs taped in Jimi's New York apartment in February 1970. All that remained was 'Scorpio Woman', recorded by Jimi during his summer 1970 trip to Maui, and inspired by his friend Melinda Merryweather, to whom he entrusted the cassette of this solo electric guitar performance. The sleeve notes referred to Jimi weaving "a host of fertile melodies throughout the song's embryonic structure". And indeed fragments of 'Midnight Lightning', 'Heaven Has No Sorrow' and 'Stepping Stone' were recognisable among the lazy, gentle guitar noodling – interrupted at one point by a ringing phone. Like 'Keep On Groovin', however, this intimate performance was no more than mildly diverting beyond an initial listen.

The Baggy's Rehearsal Sessions

Dagger 088-112-956-2 (US), July 2002

TRACKS: Burning Desire/Hoochie Coochie Man/Message To Love/Ezy Ryder/Power Of Soul/Earth Blues/Changes/Lover Man/We Gotta Live Together/Baggy's Jam/Earth Blues/Burning Desire

WHILE PREPARING FOR THEIR QUARTET OF FILLMORE EAST LIVE SHOWS AT YEAR'S end, the Band Of Gypsys booked a rehearsal space at Baggy's Studios, New York in December 1969. As ever, Hendrix ensured that proceedings were taped; and 33 years later this unassuming document from the Baggy's get-together took its place in the Dagger Records catalogue of mail-order/internet releases.

Unbeknown to collectors, the first two tracks on the album had actually been released before, on the lackustre *Loose Ends* LP, which was scarcely an advertisement for this set.

However *The Baggy's Rehearsal Sessions* proved to have unexpected depths. Filled with humour, passion and collective spirit, these live-in-the-studio takes were occasionally flawed but still infinitely more appealing than the official *Band Of Gypsys* album. Without an audience to pander to, Hendrix, Miles and Cox concentrated on turning each other on, and living up to the loose but funky potential of their material. In particular, 'Earth Blues' (especially version two) and 'Ezy Ryder' never sounded sharper and more urgent than they did here, while 'Message To Love' also carried a cohesion missing from the live LP.

Not everything here was that incendiary: 'We Gotta Live Together' was a mere fragment, the second 'Burning Desire' probably unnecessary, and 'Hoochie Coochie Man' the same throwaway it had been in 1974. But anyone with a soft spot for the Band Of Gypsys and their brand of heavy funk should track this release down.

THE HERITAGE:

LIVE ALBUMS

Isle of Wight

LP release: Polydor 2302 016 (UK), November 1971
CD release: Polydor 831 313-2 (UK), March 1989

TRACKS: Midnight Lightning/Foxy Lady/Lover Man/Freedom/All Along The Watchtower/In From The Storm

JIMI'S DEATH LESS THAN THREE WEEKS AFTER THE ISLE OF WIGHT FESTIVAL EXCITED a demand for a live album from this 'farewell' performance. *Isle of Wight* was hastily assembled to satisfy this enthusiasm, but it was never issued in America – proof that the Hendrix Estate regarded it as a souvenir for those who had attended, not a full-scale Hendrix album.

In fact, engineer Eddie Kramer, when asked by Jimi's manager Mike Jeffery to concoct an album from the festival tapes, took one listen and flatly refused. Instead, the task was handed to a British engineer, Carlos Ohlms. "I thought the album was awful," Kramer explained. "While I couldn't stop its release, I told Jeffery that under no circumstances was my name to be credited or associated with it in any way." It was a sensible request on Kramer's part, as the Polydor LP granted Jimi's memory few favours. It ran to just 34 minutes, offering two classics from his back catalogue, two songs from *The Cry Of Love*, and two previously unreleased. One of those was 'Midnight Lightning', a stodgy blues-rocker which never caught fire, and also suffered from walkie-talkie announcements being picked up by Jimi's amps. It segued naturally into an equally uninspired 'Foxy Lady', and then a chaotic, if frenetic, 'Lover Man'.

A brilliant arrangement of 'Freedom', with Hendrix reworking the tired studio version into an almost orchestrated set of riffs and runs, lifted the gloom, before a scrappy 'All Along The Watchtower' reversed the balance. The album, and the gig, ended heroically, as Mitch Mitchell's drum solo led into a passionate 'In From The Storm', Hendrix redeeming some dignity and power from a concert in which he knew he'd failed. The extent of his failure only became apparent in 1991, when a home-video and then a second CD, *Live Isle of Wight '70*, were pulled from the wreckage.

Hendrix In The West

LP release: Polydor 2301 018 (UK), January 1972
CD release: Polydor 831 312-2 (UK), February 1989

TRACKS: Johnny B. Goode/Lover Man/Blue Suede Shoes/Voodoo Child (Slight Return)/God Save The Queen/Sgt. Pepper's Lonely Hearts Club Band/Little Wing/Red House

A LONGSIDE THE ARCHIVE EXCAVATIONS THAT PRODUCED *THE CRY OF LOVE* and *Rainbow Bridge*, Mike Jeffery and Eddie Kramer considered the possibility of compiling an album from Jimi's two shows at the Community Theater in Berkeley, California, on May 30, 1970. Kramer mastered the full tapes of both shows, while a movie entitled *Jimi Plays Berkeley* was released in late 1971. But Kramer decided that the concerts didn't justify LP release in their own right, and the decision to include the Berkeley performance of 'Hear My Train A-Comin'' on *Rainbow Bridge* finally scuppered plans for the live set.

In its place, Kramer picked the best remaining tracks from Berkeley, and combined them with performances from other 1969 and 1970 live shows. The three gigs immediately available to him were the Royal Albert Hall, London, from February 24, 1969; the San Diego Sports Arena, from May 24, 1969; and the Isle of Wight Festival, on August 30, 1970. So far so good; but there were legal problems regarding the ownership of the Albert Hall tapes, which had already been raided by Ember Records for the release of the Experience LP (see the Unofficial CDs section for more details). Mike Jeffery hit upon a strange solution: using the Albert Hall tracks, but pretending that they came from San Diego. 'Voodoo Child (Slight Return)' and 'Little Wing' were deliberately miscredited, an idea that worked brilliantly until the rival claimants to the Albert Hall material actually listened to *Hendrix In The West*, whereupon they slapped a lawsuit on Jeffery and his cohorts.

Those antics aside, most of *Hendrix In The West* was a worthy tribute, and some of it was brilliant. For guitar theatrics, Jimi never topped the apparently impromptu Berkeley rendition of Chuck Berry's 'Johnny B. Goode'. It has to be heard – or seen, via *Jimi Plays Berkeley* – to be believed. The album opened with the best-ever rendition of 'Lover Man', Jimi's revamp of the blues standard 'Rock Me Baby'. It was another Berkeley cut – but then so was the appallingly lame 'Blue Suede Shoes', from the pre-show rehearsals, which was to 'Johnny B. Goode' what a snail was to a cheetah. The first disguised Albert Hall cut, 'Voodoo Child (Slight Return)', was in a different league, as Hendrix almost matched the soundscape of the studio take. Another descent into bathos followed, with the Isle of Wight intro of 'God Save The Queen'/'Sgt. Pepper' – no 'Star Spangled Banner' this. Then it was back to the Albert Hall for a poignantly beautiful 'Little Wing', which for sensitivity and technique cut the Axis studio cut dead; and finally a genuine relic from San Diego, in the shape of a long, complex 'Red House', as close to definitive as any live reading of the song.

The Jimi Hendrix Concerts

(Version 1)

LP release: CBS 88592 (UK), August 1982
CD release: Media Motion Media CD 1 (UK), August 1989

TRACKS: Fire/I Don't Live Today/Red House/Stone Free/Are You Experienced?/Little Wing/Voodoo Child (Slight Return)/Bleeding Heart/Hey Joe/Wild Thing/Hear My Train A-Comin'

TEN YEARS AFTER THE LAST ALBUM OF PREVIOUSLY UNISSUED LIVE HENDRIX performances, *The Jimi Hendrix Concerts* confirmed what collectors of tapes and bootlegs had known for years – that the potential seam of top-quality concert material ran deep and rich. The impact of this double-LP was soon diminished in the CD age by the release of *Live At Winterland*, *Stages*, and *Woodstock*, but in 1982 it served to provoke the revival of interest in the 'unofficial' Hendrix catalogue which had effectively been smothered by the disasters of the mid-Seventies.

Spread across four sides, the contents made little attempt to replicate a typical Jimi Hendrix Experience performance: in fact, two of the tracks actually featured the Billy Cox/Mitch Mitchell band, rather than Mitchell and Noel Redding. But the concentration on familiar concert landmarks did hint at the intensity and power of Jimi's live work once he freed himself from the obligation to perform as a human jukebox.

The set also registered the existence of high-fidelity tapes of Hendrix's shows at the Winterland Ballroom in San Francisco during 1968. Half the album came from this venue, and although the versions of 'Fire', 'Voodoo Child (Slight Return)' and 'Wild Thing' weren't sensational, the deliciously slow 'Little Wing' was a real find. A rare performance of 'Are You Experienced?', which opened with a feedback collage that would have delighted The Velvet Underground, topped even that, but Hendrix's finest playing from these Winterland extracts surfaced on an amazing 'Hear My Train A-Comin'' – a song that reliably liberated him to explore the depths of his blues roots. Two songs came from the Royal Albert Hall show on February 24, 1969: 'Bleeding Heart' was prosaic enough, but 'Stone Free' took on mammoth proportions, as Jimi soloed into the night, almost regardless of what song he was playing, before Mitch Mitchell replied in kind. Jimi responded with a gentle flamenco passage, easing the Experience back into a chorus that had long since become irrelevant.

The remaining three tracks sampled one song apiece from San Diego in May 1969 ('I Don't Live Today', as reissued later on *Stages*); Berkeley in May 1970 (a scrappy 'Hey Joe'); and Randall's Island in July 1970 (a surprisingly short eight minutes of 'Red House', with a characteristically emotional solo).

Problems with the then-fledgling science of CD mastering forced Media Motion Media to snip vital seconds from the original running order when they prepared the first digital version in 1989, by omitting Hendrix's spoken introductions from the disc.

The Jimi Hendrix Concerts

(Version 2)

CD release: Castle CCSCD 235 (UK), February 1990

TRACKS: Fire/I Don't Live Today/Red House/Stone Free/Are You Experienced?/Little Wing/Voodoo Child (Slight Return)/Bleeding Heart/Hey Joe/Wild Thing/Hear My Train A-Comin'/Foxy Lady

NO SOONER WAS THE MEDIA MOTION MEDIA EDITION OF THIS ALBUM IN THE shops than its status was being questioned. To avoid possible legal complications, the album was licensed by the Jimi Hendrix Estate, in the person of Alan Douglas, to Castle Communications. Their edition added one song to the original track listing – a wonderfully frenetic 'Foxy Lady' from the LA Forum on April 26, 1969.

Long since deleted, *The Jimi Hendrix Concerts* was rendered virtually irrelevant to completists by subsequent releases. Only one song here, 'Hear My Train A-Comin', from Winterland on 10 October 1968 (2nd show), has never reappeared on CD.

Johnny B. Goode

LP release: Fame FA 3160 (UK), July 1986
CD release: Capitol 432018-2 (USA), 1990

TRACKS: Voodoo Chile/All Along The Watchtower/Star Spangled Banner/
Johnny B. Goode/Machine Gun

YEARS AFTER HENDRIX'S DEATH, THE LEGAL BATTLES THAT HE INADVERTENTLY
initiated were still rumbling through the courts. The appearance of this
album on EMI-owned labels – Fame in Britain, Capitol in the States – marked
some settlement of the case between Jimi, his management and Ed
Chalpin, producer of the Curtis Knight sessions.

Designed as the soundtrack to an equally brief home-video release,
the album repeated the remarkable 'Johnny B. Goode' from *Hendrix In The
West*, added 'Machine Gun' (not found on the video) from the same Berkeley
show in May 1970, and filled out the set with three ragged performances
from Atlanta in July 1970. The 'Star Spangled Banner' from this show was a
smirk compared to the agonised wail of the Woodstock rendition and Alan
Douglas evidently thought so little of the 'All Along The Watchtower' from
Atlanta that he didn't bother to include it when devoting an entire CD to
the concert in the *Stages* box set.

Jimi Plays Monterey

Polydor 827 990-2 (UK), September 1986
Reprise 9 25358-2 (US), September 1986

TRACKS: Killing Floor/Foxy Lady/Like A Rolling Stone/Rock Me Baby/Hey
Joe/Can You See Me?/The Wind Cries Mary/Purple Haze/Wild Thing

NINETEEN YEARS AFTER THE JIMI HENDRIX EXPERIENCE MADE THEIR DÉBUT
American performance, those who weren't at the Monterey show-
grounds on June 18, 1967 were finally able to see (almost) their full show
when DA Pennebaker's Jimi Plays Monterey was unveiled at the Toronto
International Film Festival on 7 September 1986.

To coincide with that première, Polydor released this CD, which gave
an official release to a set that had been circulating via a mix of official and
bootleg recordings for years. The *Monterey Pop* film from the late Sixties
had included snippets of Jimi's set; then a 1970 LP, issued the week Hendrix
died, combined five of his Monterey songs with several by the equally ill-
fated Otis Redding.

While Pennebaker's cameras missed a song or two from the Experience's 40 minutes on stage, the audio tapes captured the entire drama. Hendrix returned to America as an unknown; he quit the Monterey stage an international star. The festival crowd had just seen The Who destroy their equipment in a bout of amphetamine-fuelled exhibitionism; now they watched aghast as Hendrix unveiled all the crowd-pleasing tracks he'd picked up during his years on the club and bar circuit.

The Monterey set opened with a crushing 'Killing Floor', fully in keeping with the contemporary rock vogue for revamped R&B standards. 'Foxy Lady' established his credentials as a flirt, before Jimi risked everything by daring to cover Bob Dylan's 'Like A Rolling Stone' – as close to a sacred object as anything in the world of 1967 rock. His reading, simultaneously cocky and restrained, was little short of a masterpiece, and after that he was home and dry. 'Rock Me Baby', a slightly nervous 'Hey Joe' and 'Can You See Me?' were punctuated with Jimi's near-embarrassing stage patter – a curious mix of naïvety and utter coolness. 'The Wind Cries Mary' and 'Purple Haze' illustrated the extremes of his artistic reach, before Jimi announced: "I'm gonna sacrifice something that I really love. Don't think I'm silly, 'cos I don't think that I'm losing my mind."

No-one in the audience could have been prepared for what followed, as Hendrix performed 'Wild Thing' – starting out with the movements of a burlesque dancer, and then metamorphosing into a shaman or a madman as he ignited his guitar, and seemed to cast spells over the audience as it burned. Roadies raced on stage to salvage the house PA; the star-packed audience howled their approval and disbelief. For once, the old clichés of overnight success were justified – and the entire episode was captured intact on the American edition of *Jimi Plays Monterey*, which retained more of the stage atmosphere and announcements than the European CD. Sadly, this historic performance has been allowed to slip out of the Hendrix catalogue in recent years, save for the inclusion of two tracks on the *Jimi Hendrix Experience* box set, although most of it is available on the 4-CD box-set, *The Monterey International Pop Festival*, Rhino/Castle, US/UK, 1992.

Live At Winterland

Polydor 833 004-2 (UK), 1988

TRACKS: Prologue/Fire/Manic Depression/Sunshine Of Your Love/Spanish Castle Magic/Red House/Killing Floor/Tax Free/Foxy Lady/Hey Joe/Purple Haze/Wild Thing/Epilogue

OVER THREE NIGHTS AND SIX SHOWS AT THE WINTERLAND BALLROOM in San Francisco, Jimi Hendrix, Noel Redding and Mitch Mitchell created some of the most magnificent, and sometimes unfocused, music of their joint career. The concerts ran twice nightly on October 10-12, 1968, coinciding with the release of *Electric Ladyland*, and the same sense of ambition that soaked the studio record also infused the live shows. But even allowing for a cameo appearance by Jefferson Airplane's Jack Casady on bass for one show, Hendrix didn't have the musical support or the studio overdubbing facilities to reproduce the sonic voyages of *Ladyland* on stage. Instead, he and his rhythm section explored the dynamics of the power trio – wavering dangerously close to the line between extravagance and excess which their rivals, Cream, crossed more often than not in 1968.

No songs were picked from the first show of the season, but the second allowed Casady to pummel his rib-bending bass-lines in time-honoured style on a chaotic but dutifully intense 'Killin' Floor', while the three-piece butchered (appropriately enough) Cream's 'Sunshine Of Your Love' as a gesture to Clapton, Baker and Bruce's recent decision to disband. The first show from the next night (October 11), provided a mostly magnificent 'Red House' – the cavils aroused by the rhythm section, whose overactive playing undercut Hendrix's blues licks. At the second house, Jimi treated 'Fire' like a plaything, letting the guitar speak the chorus as the rhythm duo struggled to keep pace. 'Tax Free' veered between genius and disaster, while Hendrix turned 'Foxy Lady' into a joyous feeding frenzy of feedback. It was obviously a wild night.

A long triple-play was taken from the first show on the 12th – Hendrix pumping his guitar into pomp-rock cacophony before lurching into 'Hey Joe', then 'Purple Haze' and finally 'Wild Thing'. The last gig of the residency added a fine 'Manic Depression', and a theatrical 'Spanish Castle Magic'. The overall result? A narrow but thrilling victory for artistic nerve over sheer exuberance. 'Spanish Castle Magic' and 'Foxy Lady' both exposed the limitations of the original tape source: there again, who wanted pure digital sound from Hendrix in '68? Sharp-eared consumers should note that Rykodisc prepared a 'gold disc' CD edition of *Live At Winterland* for the US market, supposedly guaranteeing even better sound. Both versions have long since been deleted, however.

Live At Winterland +3

Rykodisc RCD 20038+3 (USA), September 1992

TRACKS: Full contents of above release, plus bonus tracks on CD single: Are You Experienced?/Voodoo Child (Slight Return)/Like A Rolling Stone

I F THE CASH-CRAZY EXPLOITERS OF THE NINETIES HAD BEEN LET LOOSE ON THE Sixties, what fun they could have had. How about two different editions of *Electric Ladyland*, one with the long 'Voodoo Chile', the other with 'Voodoo Child (Slight Return)', so that true fans would have to buy both?

Some of that self-serving marketing spirit was exhibited when Rykodisc, who had issued the original *Live At Winterland* in the States, prepared a special commemorative edition of the CD four years later. Inside a box with the CD was a T-shirt (whoopee) and a three-track CD single, featuring performances that weren't available anywhere else. Even allowing for the fact that the three songs ran to 30 minutes – 12 of 'Like A Rolling Stone' (with Herbie Rich on organ), 14 of 'Are You Experienced?' – this was a particularly shabby trick, especially when the entire package retailed for $40. All the new tracks were taken from October 11 – two from the first show, 'Like A Rolling Stone' from the second.

Radio One

(Version 1)

Castle CCSCD 212 (UK), February 1989

TRACKS: Stone Free/Radio One/Day Tripper/Killin' Floor/Love Or Confusion/Drivin' South/Catfish Blues/Wait Until Tomorrow/Getting My Heart Back Together Again/Hound Dog/Fire/I'm Your Hoochie Coochie Man*(sic)*/Purple Haze/Spanish Castle Magic/Hey Joe/Foxy Lady/The Burning Of The Midnight Lamp

A DECADE BEFORE THE RELEASE OF *BBC SESSIONS*, *RADIO ONE* OFFERED THE first ever official glimpse of Hendrix's adventures with the British Broadcasting Corporation. It featured 17 tracks, while an additional two were available on tie-in releases. The track selection wasn't entirely uncontroversial, as many diehards wanted to see Hendrix's cover of Bob Dylan's 'Can You Please Crawl Out Your Window' preserved for posterity, but what was included was still more than sufficient to attract copious critical plaudits.

The flat ambience of the BBC studios worked its usual dampening act even on The Jimi Hendrix Experience, giving these recordings a thinner sound than his other 1967 output. That problem aside, the presentation of *Radio One* was commendable – though two tracks were slightly miscredited (see below), and the sleeve-notes repeated the 15-year-old myth that John Lennon had been in the studio to assist the Experience with their rather scrappy cover of The Beatles' 'Day Tripper'. Incidentally, Rykodisc in the States, who issued this set just before Castle in Britain, also prepared a picture CD edition.

Radio One

(Version 2)

Victor VDP 1454 (Japan) c. 1990

TRACKS: Stone Free/Radio One/Day Tripper/Killin' Floor/Love Or Confusion/Drivin' South/Catfish Blues/Wait Until Tomorrow/Getting My Heart Back Together Again/Hound Dog/Fire/I'm Your Hoochie Coochie Man *(sic)*/Purple Haze/Spanish Castle Magic/Hey Joe/Foxey Lady/The Burning Of The Midnight Lamp/Hear My Train A-Comin'/Drivin' South

THE JAPANESE RELEASE OF THE BBC SESSIONS ADDED THE TWO FINAL TRACKS, both borrowed from the US 'Day Tripper' CD single. Though Rykodisc claimed that they had never been broadcast in the Sixties, it was actually the versions on the original *Radio One* line-up that were the out-takes.

Footlights

Polydor 847 235-2 (UK), February 1991

Comprised new *Isle Of Wight* & *Band Of Gypsys* CDs, plus *Live At Winterland* & *Jimi Plays Monterey*

FOOTLIGHTS UNVEILED THE 'NEW' VERSIONS OF THE *BAND OF GYPSYS* AND *Isle Of Wight* CDs in Britain for the first time. Thankfully, both were also available separately, preventing loyal fans from having to duplicate the *Winterland* and *Monterey* sets.

Live Isle Of Wight '70

Polydor 847 236-2 (UK), June 1991

TRACKS: Intro/God Save The Queen/Message To Love/Voodoo Chile/Lover Man/Machine Gun/Dolly Dagger/Red House/In From The Storm/New Rising Sun

I HAVE A PROBLEM WITH THE WHOLE SET," EXPLAINED ALAN DOUGLAS WHEN HE was quizzed about his plans for the Isle of Wight tapes. "With a film, it's OK. As a record, there's no new interesting tracks on it." However 1991 still saw the release of a home-video and a live CD, both documenting a performance that Eddie Kramer described as "awful", and Hendrix himself regarded with some degree of anguish, as the video made clear.

Much of that confusion was captured on the first 'official' CD record of the show, which replaced the strictly UK-only *Isle Of Wight* album. ("That has all the wrong songs on it," was Douglas's comment on that first attempt.) Alan Douglas' track selection didn't offer Jimi too many favours, omitting (for example) by far the strongest track on *Isle Of Wight*, 'Freedom', but retaining the lacklustre opening salvo of 'God Save The Queen'. As usual, the running order of the original show was abandoned in favour of a more listenable revamp. For similar reasons, Mitch Mitchell's drum solo was edited out of the majestic 'In From The Storm', one of the few survivors from the previous CD. Left in, though, was Jimi's tell-tale chat, which clearly revealed his dissatisfaction with the sound, his guitar, his state of mind and the audience; and the accidental walkie-talkie chatter picked up over the PA during 'Machine Gun', which is exactly what was pissing Jimi off.

Stages

Polydor 511 763-2 (UK), February 1992

TRACKS:
CD1: Sgt. Pepper's Lonely Hearts Club Band/Fire/The Wind Cries Mary/Foxy Lady/Hey Joe/I Don't Live Today/The Burning Of The Midnight Lamp/Purple Haze
CD2: Killing Floor/Catfish Blues/Foxy Lady/Red House/Drivin' South/Tune-Up Song (Spanish Castle Magic)/The Wind Cries Mary/Fire/Little Wing/Purple Haze
CD3: Fire/Hey Joe/Spanish Castle Magic/Red House/I Don't Live Today/Purple Haze/Voodoo Child (Slight Return)
CD4: Fire/Lover Man/Spanish Castle Magic/Foxy Lady/Purple

TWENTY-ONE YEARS AFTER JIMI HENDRIX'S DEATH, THE TREATMENT OF HIS back catalogue had become more controversial than at any time since the mid-Seventies. The fans demanded authenticity – undubbed, unedited studio out-takes, and full-length live shows. The Estate, then operated by Alan Douglas' Are You Experienced Ltd., were still attempting to remake Hendrix in their own image. Within that dispute, *Stages* was a definite compromise from Douglas. Though it was by no means perfect, few of the posthumous Jimi releases had been greeted with such unanimous delight by fans and collectors alike.

The project grew out of a late-Eighties plan to release a *Best Of The Bootlegs* CD. As Douglas and his team began to sift through potential inclusions, they realised that something more substantial could easily be created. "The name Stages is a double entendre," Douglas told *ICE* magazine. "He's on stage, and these are the stages of his evolution as a guitar player during those four years."

The theory was simple enough: to present four complete Hendrix shows, one from each year from 1967 to 1970. 1967 was represented by the Experience (Jimi, Noel and Mitch) in Studio 4 of Stockholm's Radiohuset, for a live broadcast on September 5, that year. For 1968, Douglas dug up the much-bootlegged tapes of the Experience at the Paris Olympia four months later – on January 29, to be exact. The 1969 show was from San Diego Sports Arena on May 24, with the Experience at one of their final shows. Finally, 1970's offering was taped in Atlanta, on July 4, with Billy Cox and Mitch Mitchell.

At Stockholm, the Experience were still confined by the conventions of the era – that is, no unseemly jamming, nothing too unfamiliar in the repertoire, and a fair smattering of hit singles in the set. There were moments, notably on 'I Don't Live Today', when their internal cohesion came close to collapse, while the tentative introduction to 'The Burning Of The Midnight Lamp' revealed that this was their first live rendition of the song. But 'Midnight Lamp' gradually grew in confidence, and the set ended with a tumultuous 'Purple Haze', as Jimi coaxed barbaric howls from his guitar, and then slid from the barrage of feedback into the loping riff that underpinned the song.

Within a few months, the Experience were in Paris, delivering a set that could hardly have been more different. The pop ambience of the '67 show was gone, and in its place Hendrix asserted his blues roots – opening with a remarkable double whammy of Howlin' Wolf's 'Killing Floor' and Muddy Waters' 'Catfish Blues', the latter clearly signalling the imminent arrival of Jimi's own 'Voodoo Chile'. The set also included a fine 'Red House', while the instrumental 'Drivin' South' might not have matched the fury of the *Radio One* rendition, but still added another layer of potent rock guitar to a compelling concert. Once again, Jimi climaxed with an ocean of sound and 'Purple Haze'.

Fast forward another year and the Experience were treading water. San Diego in 1969 was a step into the past, as Jimi returned to his back catalogue for 'Fire' and 'Hey Joe'. An intricate 'Spanish Castle Magic' led briefly into 'Sunshine Of Your Love', while a slow, spacey 'Red House' (first heard on *Hendrix In The West*) was the show's finest moment. It was rivalled by 'I Don't Live Today' (premièred on *The Jimi Hendrix Concerts*), the foundation for some stunning sonic experimentation. But the closing flurry of 'Purple Haze' and 'Voodoo Child' (interrupted by the exuberance of the crowd) couldn't quite extend that mood.

Where the crowd led in '69, Hendrix, Billy Cox and Mitch Mitchell followed a year later. The Independence Day show in Atlanta proved either (a) that Jimi loved performing that summer and cast all his musical inhibitions to the wind or (b) that he felt so trapped by the constant demands of his international audience that he made little effort to disguise his contempt and boredom. Or possibly (c): both of the above.

'Fire' was the case for the defence, as Hendrix romped through a rendition of the song that swamped the '67 attempt. Ditto 'Spanish Castle Magic', with its long, playful solo. But 'Hear My Train A-Comin'', despite being stretched to 10 minutes in search of inspiration, never matched (for example) the beauty of the take on *Rainbow Bridge*, while 'Stone Free' was a stone mess from start to finish. The key evidence was 'Star Spangled Banner' – the 1969 Woodstock version a soulful cry of despair at America's political direction, at Atlanta a year later the vehicle for four minutes of guitar hysterics that had all the reverence of a whoopee cushion in a cathedral. From there, 'Straight Ahead' and 'Room Full Of Mirrors' were no more than throwaways and even 'Voodoo Child (Slight Return)' couldn't survive the show's slaphappy, carefree spirit.

Collectors complained that at least three of the four concerts on *Stages* weren't taken from the best sources; that the order of the 1967 and 1970 songs had been altered, for no apparent reason; and that the 1969 and 1970 shows were incomplete. In particular, the disappearance of 'Foxy Lady' from San Diego was baffling, as it would easily have fitted onto the CD. Another complaint was sparked by the San Diego take of 'I Don't Live Today', which now ran shorter than on its original LP appearance a decade earlier.

For the novice, the sound quality of all four shows fell some way short of 'professional' expectations, with the Paris 1968 gig especially muddy. But the sheer historical and musical value of the set far outweighed these considerations.

EXP Over Sweden

Univibes UV 1002 (Ireland), January 1994

TRACKS: Can You See Me?/Killing Floor/Foxy Lady/Catfish Blues/Hey Joe/Fire/The Wind Cries Mary/Purple Haze/EXP/Up From The Skies/Little Wing/I Don't Live Today

THE SECOND SUBSCRIBERS-ONLY PACKAGE FROM THE EXCELLENT *UNIVIBES* Hendrix fanzine, *EXP Over Sweden* sampled four Swedish performances from four separate Experience tours. For hardcore collectors, this warts-and-all undertaking was far preferable to the sanitised, mass-marketed exercises of the official Estate; but for the general public, the source tapes raided for this project would have proved a little too basic for easy listening.

The album opened with an outdoor recording of 'Can You See Me?' from the Tivoli Gardens in Stockholm on May 24, 1967 – a wild performance, undercut only by the defiantly lo-fi recording quality. From the same venue, but this time an indoor concert hall, we moved forward to September 4, 1967, and a seven-song set that was prey to every form of distortion imaginable – hiss, buzz, wow, flutter, compression, sheer noise – but still delivered an explosive 'Killing Floor', another delta excursion through 'Catfish Blues', then the usual run of hits climaxing in a feedback-strewn 'Purple Haze'.

Four months later, the Experience were back in Stockholm for a show at the Konserthuset, where they unveiled a rare – possibly even unique – live performance of the opening flurry of the *Axis: Bold As Love* album, the coupling of 'EXP' and 'Up From The Skies', followed by 'Little Wing'. It was a brave, doomed, but still majestic attempt to capture the studio trickery of the LP in a live show, but it suffered from sound quality poorer than any other tracks listed in this book.

Finally, the set skipped forward exactly a year, but moved from Stockholm to Gothenburg, where the Experience treated 'I Don't Live Today' to an eight-minute excursion – complete with lengthy drum intro from Mitch Mitchell, and some neat quotes from 'Third Stone From The Sun' during Hendrix's solo. With its A5 colour booklet detailing the performances with almost too much technical precision, and a sheaf of rare photos of Hendrix in Sweden, this was an essential purchase for those who valued musical content over sound quality.

Woodstock

MCA MCACD 11063 (UK), July 1994

TRACKS: Introduction/Fire/Izabella/Hear My Train A-Comin'/Red House/Jam Back At The House/Voodoo Child (Slight Return)/Stepping Stone/Star Spangled Banner/Purple Haze/Woodstock Improvisation/Villanova Junction/Farewell

"JIMI'S GREATEST PERFORMANCE": THAT WAS HOW MCA MARKETED THIS CD, cunningly issued to catch the tidal wave of Woodstock 25th anniversary hype, and just one of half-a-dozen cash-in – oops, sorry, tie-in – albums which were thrown at the nostalgia-hungry public in time for Woodstock '94.

For about 15, maybe 20 minutes of his show, the Hendrix hype was justified (see *Live At Woodstock* for full details). The earlier *:Woodstock* (yes, that *:Blues* colon again) captures most of what was essential from the concert, though it trimmed a couple of minutes from 'Stepping Stone', and pretended that the closing 'Hey Joe' never happened. Indeed, Alan Douglas's track selection mangled the order of the first five songs on the CD, and rejected the opportunity to present the entire tangled Woodstock performance. Even the opening applause was clearly overdubbed as a tape loop, reappearing at inappropriate moments throughout the album. Only the lengthy liner notes represented anything of a saving grace on a disappointingly lacklustre package.

Jimi In Denmark

UniVibes UV 1003 (Ireland), January 1995

TRACKS: Catfish Blues/Tax Free/Master James & Co./Fire/Voodoo Child (Slight Return)/Foxy Lady/Spanish Castle Magic/Freedom

IN THE DYING DAYS OF THE ALAN DOUGLAS REGIME, UNIVIBES WERE ALLOWED a third and last (after *Calling Long Distance* and *EXP Over Sweden*) trip into the Hendrix vaults for the benefit of their loyal subscribers. Casual listeners might well conclude that only such loyal subscribers could have had the patience to endure such a lo-fi collection of audience recordings from Jimi's various Copenhagen shows. But this was one occasion where patience was rewarded.

A wildly intense reading of 'Catfish Blues' from January 7, 1968 opened the proceedings, followed by one of the most extreme guitar extravaganzas of Hendrix's career: the instrumental 'Tax Free' from the first show on January 10, 1969. The degree of interplay between the band was tough to judge, as all that came through the speakers was guitar. Jimi obviously relished the open spaces but defining structure of this tune, and he pulled the Experience through a series of carefully controlled rushes and climaxes. One minute he was unreeling delicate Latin-esque passing chords; the next he was stretching and hammering the familiar 'Foxy Lady' riff to the point of mania. It was an utterly phenomenal performance.

From the second show that same day came a fairly standard set of 'Fire', 'Voodoo Child' and 'Foxy Lady', but 'Spanish Castle Magic' was something else. Jimi trashed the well-worn path through the song, opting instead for a long diversion through ear-threatening feedback sustain, while Noel and Mitch pummelled and pulse behind him like Machiavellian subversives. Eventually the trio drifted into an improvised slow movement, as Hendrix toyed with a variety of half-remembered themes, before coherence and planning returned, and the band finally found their way back to base. Like 'Tax Free', this was essential listening, regardless of the dubious sound quality. Not so the closing 'Freedom', however, from September 1970, which paled alongside the definitive Isle of Wight rendition.

The mysterious 'Master James & Co' was a 23-minute interview – or more accurately confrontation – taped between the two 1969 shows. For once, Jimi's natural politeness failed him; while Noel Redding endlessly complained about the lack of beer backstage Hendrix took the hapless questioner to task for the banality of his enquiries. "Interviewers should have a little more imagination today," he chided the journalist, rather than forcing him to keep "jabbering about the past". It was an amusing listen in the spirit of *schadenfreude*, but short on factual or musical insight.

Live At The Oakland Coliseum

Dagger DBRD2-11743 (US), February 1998

TRACKS:
CD1: Introduction/Fire/Hey Joe/Spanish Castle Magic/Hear My Train A-Comin'/Sunshine Of Your Love/Red House
CD2: Foxy Lady/Star Spangled Banner/Purple Haze/Voodoo Child (Slight Return)

THE SUCCESS OF THE GRATEFUL DEAD'S SERIES OF ARCHIVE LIVE RECORDINGS, known collectively as *Dick's Picks*, triggered a flurry of similar projects among the controllers of other potentially lucrative catalogues. Experience Hendrix have taken flak for some of their marketing exercises and creative decisions. But the formation of the mail-order/internet label, Dagger Records, has been greeted warmly throughout the Hendrix community.

Dagger, so the company explained on this debut release, was "a unique label we have established to bring Jimi's fans inspired performances that don't meet the technical recording criteria and sonic high standards Hendrix himself established over the course of his short but spectacular career. Releases on Dagger Records are not intended for the casual fan. If you haven't experienced groundbreaking Hendrix albums like *Are You Experienced* and *Electric Ladyland*, you shouldn't be listening to this album yet … Dagger Records plans to service the healthy demand for Jimi's music with informative 'bootleg' releases which are properly annotated, complete with photos and reasonable sonic quality." Just in case we still hadn't got the message, the back cover added: "Warning! This amateur, monophonic recording does not represent the usual stereo fidelity of live concert recordings."

In the case of the Jimi Hendrix Experience at the Oakland Coliseum in California on April 27, 1969, the amateur taper was Hendrix fan Ken Koga, who recorded the show on a portable reel-to-reel machine from the eleventh row of the stalls – pausing between songs to conserve tape, and thereby missing most of the stage chatter. A day earlier, the Experience had played the L.A. Forum show heard on *Lifelines*; up the coast, in one of America's most turbulent communities, the home of the Black Panther Party, Hendrix, Redding and Mitchell delivered another explosive show.

The repertoire – captured in lo-fi but still thrilling quality on Koga's tape – was typical of the 1969 tour: an almost unduly enthusiastic 'Fire', a brooding 'Hey Joe', and then arguably the wildest 'Spanish Castle Magic' ever committed to tape, with Hendrix exploring the lower reaches of his guitar with unchained ferocity. 'Hear My Train A-Comin'' matched its intensity, but 'Sunshine Of Your Love' sounded more tentative and exploratory. Maybe the Experience were simply regrouping their energy, as 'Red House' was phenomenal – slow, brooding and free-flowing. It was clearly one of those nights, as even 'Foxy Lady' burned into a lengthy jam session.

After that, 'Star Spangled Banner' was played so straight at first that it must have been difficult to distinguish the irony, until Hendrix began to dismantle the melody in the second verse. 'Purple Haze' emerged from the sonic chaos, as usual, before Jimi introduced Jefferson Airplane bassist Jack Casady for a closing journey through 'Voodoo Child (Slight Return)'. Few Sixties rock performers could match Casady's sheer musicality, but he was left sprawling in Hendrix's wake as the four-man Experience jammed on. After such an epic performance, Jimi can be forgiven for confusing his bassists and thanking "Jack Bruce" at the end of the show.

Live At Clark University

Dagger DBRD-12033 (US), July 1999

TRACKS: Jimi Hendrix Pre-Concert Interview/Fire/Red House/Foxy Lady/Purple Haze/Wild Thing/Noel Redding Post-Concert Interview/Mitch Mitchell Post-Concert Interview/Jimi Hendrix Post-Concert Interview

FILM-MAKER TONY PALMER TRAVELLED TO WORCESTER, MASSACHUSETTS, ON 15 March 1968 to capture The Experience for his rather mannered BBC-TV documentary, *All My Loving*. He conducted lengthy interviews with the group both before and after the second show of the night, and also filmed that performance – though the five songs included on this second Dagger release actually come from another unrevealed source, and have survived in surprisingly good stereo.

Musically, this was simply another night on the road, as the Experience trawled one more time through their standard repertoire. Once the initial vocal distortion cleared, 'Fire' made for an exciting opener, while 'Foxy Lady' was already showing signs of developing from a theatrical crowd-pleaser into a vehicle for jamming. The taper missed the opening of an erratic 'Purple Haze', but caught a deliberately self-parodic 'Wild Thing' in full, as Hendrix dragged in his usual repertoire of borrowed licks, from 'Blue Moon' to Western movie themes.

But the real interest here is provided by the interviews, which run for more than 40 minutes in total. By 1968 standards, the Experience's responses were uniformly intelligent, as Hendrix waxed lyrical about the nature of music, Redding debunked the myth of stardom, and Mitchell chimed in with a rap about the gulf between pop hype and reality. Beneath the enthusiasm, though, Hendrix clearly revealed his impatience with his current image: "Anybody could get tired of playing 'Purple Haze' every night".

Live In Ottawa

Dagger 088-112-737-2 (US), October 2001

TRACKS: Killing Floor/Tax Free/Fire/Red House/Foxy Lady/Hey Joe/Spanish Castle Magic/Purple Haze/Wild Thing

FOUR DAYS AFTER THEIR ENCOUNTER WITH TONY PALMER AT CLARK UNIVERSITY, and two days after Jimi's much-bootlegged jam at New York's Café Au Go Go, the Experience slipped over the Canadian border to the Capitol Theater. The night's second show survived on what Dagger call "a raw, two-track mixing console recording" which, they speculate, was running at Hendrix's instruction – or, at the very least, with his knowledge. The result was a bootleg quality document that captured both the excitement and the limitations of Experience live shows in 1968.

Hendrix was a notoriously self-effacing and apologetic performer, and he regularly had to make amends for the amplification systems he encountered on the road. "I hate to bring my own self down with this raggedy equipment", he complained after the propulsive opening of 'Killing Floor', during which the sonic picture went through a series of abrupt changes. The instrumental 'Tax Free' opened as if Jimi was still distracted, but a couple of minutes in, the music took control, as he steered the band through a compelling series of mini-climaxes that subverted the basic structure of the tune. After that musical exploration, 'Fire' (bedevilled by foreign noises in the speakers) seemed forced, and Jimi introduced 'Red House' like a man who'd rather be somewhere else entirely. But he used the expansive terrain of his blues anthem to play himself back into spirits – though at times he lost touch with his rhythm section, as if he was playing out some personal psychodrama with the music.

The remainder of the set proceeded on a more even keel, though an apology was rarely far from Jimi's lips, and his guitar veered dangerously out of tune as the band entered the finale of 'Wild Thing'. Midway through that song, the tape ran out, as if echoing his waning enthusiasm for the whole Experience.

Voodoo Chile. *(LFI)*

Jimi in Zurich for the Beat Monsters concert, May 1968, with
(l-r) Carl Wayne (The Move), Steve Winwood (Traffic), John Mayall
(John Mayall's Bluesbreakers) and Eric Burdon (The Animals). *(LFI)*

Jimi behind the drums at the
Zurich rehearsals, May 1968. *(LFI)*

Jimi with trademark Stratocaster,
which he played by flipping it
upside down. *(LFI)*

The sleeve to *Smash Hits*, the first of numerous Hendrix compilations (1968).

On stage, US tour, October 1968. *(LFI)*

Band Of Gypsies sleeve (1970).

The Cry Of Love sleeve, 1971.

Jimi (with Noel Redding in the background) onstage at the
Royal Albert Hall, February 1969, towards the end of the
original Experience. *(LFI)*

Live at Woodstock, August 1969. *(Henry Diltz/Corbis)*

Hendrix with road manager Eric Barrett arriving at Heathrow Airport on the way to the Isle of Wight festival, August 1970. *(Bettmann/Corbis)*

Jimi on stage at the Isle of Wight festival, August 1970. His uninspired performance was to be his last show in the UK. *(LFI)*

Cornerstones, a 1990 compilation.

Experience Hendrix: The Best Of Jimi Hendrix, a TV advertised collection from 2000.

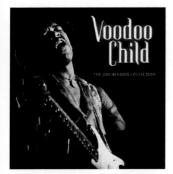

Voodoo Chile: The Jimi Hendrix Collection (2002). The Hendrix legend thrives thanks to the continuation of such archive releases from the official Experience Hendrix estate.

Jimi Hendrix: No More A Rolling Stone (2004) Just one of hundreds of unofficial Hendrix titles to flood the marketplace.

Ezy Rider. More than 34 years after his premature passing
Jimi Hendrix's place as one of the most influential artists of the
20th century remains secure. *(LFI)*

Paris 1967/
San Francisco 1968

Dagger CATF 05056-2 (US), April 2003

TRACKS: Stone Free/Hey Joe/Fire/Rock Me Baby/Red House/Purple Haze/Wild Thing/Killing Floor/Red House/Catfish Blues/Dear Mr. Fantasy (Part One)/Dear Mr. Fantasy (Part Two)/Purple Haze

PROOF OF DAGGER'S COMMENDABLE SENSE OF ETHICS CAME ON THIS ALBUM, which coupled two shows taped four months apart. A less scrupulous company would have offered the Paris Olympia show from 9 October, 1967 as a CD in itself; instead, Dagger included the remaining releasable tracks from a radio recording that had already been sampled on the *Jimi Hendrix Experience* box set. To fill out the CD, they added five songs (but six tracks) from the second show at the Winterland Ballroom in San Francisco on February 4, 1968, taken from a stereo soundboard.

Hendrix had been an icon in Paris since his first appearance at the Olympia a year earlier and comments such as "Vive la France, right? Yeah!" only added to the fervour of the crowd. A propulsive 'Stone Free' was followed by a chaotic but inspired 'Hey Joe', and a version of 'Fire' delivered, for once, with unfeigned enthusiasm. It wouldn't have been an Experience show without technical problems, however, and the remainder of the gig was a duet between raucous energy and sonic chaos. "Do you remember that one?" Hendrix asked as he introduced 'Rock Me Baby'. "Cos I've forgotten."

By the time they reached California the following year, the Experience had revamped their repertoire. The tape opened with 'Killing Floor' in progress, and an unusually frantic 'Red House' about to begin. After a slow and stately 'Catfish Blues', Mitch Mitchell generously made way for Electric Flag percussionist Buddy Miles to take his place. The taping was interrupted during the subsequent jam through Traffic's 'Dear Mr. Fantasy', with Miles adding a granite-thick rhythm in place of Mitchell's jazzier playing, and Hendrix responding to the novelty with intensity and focus. With the normal Experience service resumed, the trio slipped into a finale of 'Purple Haze', featuring a Hendrix vocal of rare intensity – the close of a fascinating document of a unique performance.

THE HERITAGE:

COMPILATIONS

Smash Hits

(Version 1)

LP release: Track 613 004 (UK), April 1968
CD release: Polydor 825 255-2 (UK), February 1985

TRACKS: Purple Haze/Fire/The Wind Cries Mary/Can You See Me?/51st
Anniversary/Hey Joe/Stone Free/The Stars That Play With Laughing Sam's
Dice/Manic Depression/Highway Chile/The Burning Of The Midnight
Lamp/Foxy Lady

DURING WHAT WAS, BY SIXTIES' STANDARDS, A LENGTHY PAUSE BETWEEN
the release of *Axis: Bold As Love* at the end of 1967 and *Electric Ladyland*
almost a year later, Track Records in England grew perturbed by the suggestion that the record-buying public might forget who Jimi Hendrix was. To
maintain his profile, they hastily assembled *Smash Hits* for the British market, with its stunning triple-exposure cover almost overshadowed by the
crass, comic-style lettering. Nothing on the album was new, but it did at
least collect together Jimi's pre-1968 non-LP singles.

In the first stirrings of the CD era, Polydor were quite happy to transfer
fifth-generation tapes onto a disgustingly poor compact disc. It was hard to
know where the criticisms should begin: the back cover and booklet shot of
Jimi apparently playing guitar right-handed, the atrocious sound quality
(check the almost unlistenable reproduction of the stoned mayhem of 'The
Stars That Play With Laughing Sam's Dice') or the fact that the CD clipped
the first half-second off at least three tracks, 'Fire', 'The Wind Cries Mary' and
'Stone Free'. This was easily the worst CD ever to appear in the 'official'
Hendrix catalogue.

Smash Hits

(Version 2)

LP release: Reprise MS 2025 (USA), July 1969
CD release: Reprise 2776-2 (USA), 1985

TRACKS: Purple Haze/Fire/The Wind Cries Mary/Can You See Me?/Hey Joe/Stone Free/Manic Depression/Foxy Lady/Crosstown Traffic/All Along The Watchtower/Red House/Remember/51st Anniversary/Highway Chile

AMERICA MISSED OUT ON THE FIRST TRANSFER OF *SMASH HITS* TO CD, FOR which it should be grateful. By 1989, digital remastering made this set a much more attractive option than its UK counterpart – especially for those with CD Video players, as the Hendrix Estate's engineers had added video graphics to the delights of the music.

The track listing added '51st Anniversary' and 'Highway Chile' to the original US line-up of the LP – though not 'The Stars That Play With Laughing Sam's Dice', which never appeared in America during Jimi's lifetime. Its inclusion on this CD would have neatly collected all the original Experience A- and B-sides on one package.

Smash Hits

(Version 3)

MCA 112 984-2 (US), September 2002

TRACKS: Purple Haze/Fire/The Wind Cries Mary/Can You See Me?/Hey Joe/All Along The Watchtower/Stone Free/ Crosstown Traffic/Manic Depression/Remember/Red House/Foxy Lady

Smash Hits

(Version 4)

MCA 113 007-2 (UK), September 2002

TRACKS: Purple Haze/Fire/The Wind Cries Mary/Can You See Me?/51st Anniversary/Hey Joe/Stone Free/The Stars That Play With Laughing Sam's Dice/Manic Depression/Highway Chile/The Burning Of The Midnight Lamp/Foxy Lady

W ITH ALL THE POTENTIAL BONUS TRACKS ALREADY AVAILABLE ON THE *Are You Experienced* CD, the Estate opted to revert to the original track listings from 1968 (UK) and 1969 (USA) – albeit with easily the best sound reproduction to date. There were no sleeve-notes, but the hysterical 'cowboy' photo (from the US version) spreads more than compensated.

Soundtrack Recordings From The Film 'Jimi Hendrix'

LP release: Reprise K 64017 (UK), June 1973
Unissued on CD

TRACKS: Rock Me Baby/Wild Thing/Machine Gun/Johnny B. Goode/Hey Joe/Purple Haze/Like A Rolling Stone/Star Spangled Banner/Machine Gun/Hear My Train A-Comin'/Red House/In From The Storm plus interviews

E SSENTIALLY A LIVE 'GREATEST HITS' SET, TAKEN FROM THE TAPES IN professional circulation at the time the album was released, this double-LP accompanied *A Film About Jimi Hendrix* – the excellent (for the period) documentary movie assembled by Joe Boyd in 1972/73. Alongside many of the interview clips used in the film, the album contained 'Rock Me Baby', 'Wild Thing', 'Hey Joe' and 'Like A Rolling Stone' from Monterey in June 1967 (all later included on *Jimi Plays Monterey*); the beautiful acoustic 'Hear My Train A-Comin' from December 1967 (on the *:Blues* CD); 'Star Spangled Banner' from Woodstock in 1969; 'Machine Gun' from *Band Of Gypsys*;

'Johnny B. Goode' from Berkeley in May 1970 (now on the Jimi Hendrix Experience box); 'Purple Haze' from the same show (the solitary track never issued on CD); and 'In From The Storm', 'Red House' and 'Machine Gun' from the Isle of Wight in August 1970 (all available on *Blue Wild Angel*).

The Essential
Jimi Hendrix

Volumes One And Two

LP releases: Volume One, Polydor 2612 034 (UK), August 1978;
Volume Two, Polydor 2311 014 (UK), January 1981
CD release: Reprise 26035-2 (USA), November 1989

TRACKS: Are You Experienced?/Third Stone From The Sun/Purple Haze/Hey Joe/Fire/Foxy Lady/The Wind Cries Mary/Little Wing/If Six Was Nine/Bold As Love/Little Miss Lover/Castles Made Of Sand/Gypsy Eyes/The Burning Of The Midnight Lamp/Voodoo Child (Slight Return)/Crosstown Traffic/Still Raining, Still Dreaming/Have You Ever Been (To Electric Ladyland)?/All Along The Watchtower/House Burning Down/Room Full Of Mirrors/Izabella/Freedom/Dolly Dagger/Stepping Stone/Drifting/Ezy Ryder/Wild Thing/Machine Gun/Star Spangled Banner/Gloria

*T*HE *ESSENTIAL JIMI HENDRIX* WAS A DOUBLE-LP, *VOLUME TWO* A SINGLE affair, and their obvious purpose was to present an anthology to replace the outdated *Smash Hits*. As an incentive to collectors, the first volume was originally accompanied by a one-sided single featuring a long (but still edited) cover of Van Morrison's 'Gloria', cut during an Experience jam session at TTG Studios in October 1968. There were obvious omissions from the two albums – notably any record of 'Red House' – but they still represented a very useful introduction to Hendrix's work. One song from the vinyl releases, 'I Don't Live Today', was omitted from the CD edition.

The Singles Album

LP release: Polydor PODV 6 (UK), February 1983
CD release: Polydor 827 369-2 (Germany), April 1986

TRACKS: Hey Joe/Stone Free/Purple Haze/51st Anniversary/The Wind Cries Mary/Highway Chile/The Burning Of The Midnight Lamp/The Stars That Play With Laughing Sam's Dice/All Along The Watchtower/Long Hot Summer Night/Crosstown Traffic/Fire/Voodoo Child (Slight Return)/Angel/Night Bird Flying/Gypsy Eyes/Remember/Johnny B. Goode/Little Wing/Foxy Lady/Manic Depression/Third Stone From The Sun/Gloria

THIS SET WAS INTENDED TO INCLUDE EVERY SONG ISSUED ON A UK HENDRIX 45rpm single, both before and after his death. It didn't quite achieve its aim: missing the coupling of the acoustic 'Hear My Train A-Comin' and the Monterey 'Rock Me Baby', released in a vain attempt to promote the *Jimi Hendrix* film soundtrack LP in 1973, plus (more importantly) the US-only Band Of Gypsys single, 'Stepping Stone'/'Izabella'.

Kiss The Sky

LP release: Polydor 823 704-1 (UK), November 1984
CD release: Polydor 823 704-2 (UK), November 1984

TRACKS: Are You Experienced?/I Don't Live Today/Voodoo Child (Slight Return)/Stepping Stone/Castles Made Of Sand/Killing Floor/Purple Haze/Red House/Crosstown Traffic/Third Stone From The Sun/All Along The Watchtower

KISS THE SKY WAS AN ALAN DOUGLAS CREATION DESIGNED AS A JIMI HENDRIX primer, accentuating the sonic ebullience of his guitar playing rather than hit singles. Collectors lapped up the few seconds of studio chatter added to the take of 'Red House' originally issued on the US *Smash Hits* LP, and the presence of a slightly remixed 'Stepping Stone' from the 1970 Band Of Gypsys single. Otherwise this was familiar material all the way – with 'Killing Floor' pulled from the Monterey '67 performance, and 'I Don't Live Today' from the San Diego Sports Arena '69. This was the first Hendrix compact disc to be issued simultaneously with the vinyl edition.

The Best Of Jimi Hendrix

EMI CDP 746 485 2 (Europe), May 1987

TRACKS: Who Knows/Machine Gun/Hear My Train A-Comin'/Foxy Lady/Power To Love/Message Of Love/Voodoo Chile/Stone Free/Ezy Ryder

THIS MISLEADINGLY-TITLED ALBUM CONTAINED TRACKS FROM THE ORIGINAL *Band Of Gypsys* album ('Who Knows', 'Machine Gun', 'Power Of Love' and 'Message Of Love'), and from the inept *Band Of Gypsys 2* album. As on that LP, 'Voodoo Child (Slight Return)', 'Stone Free' and 'Ezy Ryder' weren't Band Of Gypsys performances, but live cuts from Atlanta and Berkeley in 1970.

Live And Unreleased

Castle HBCD 100 (UK), November 1989

TRACKS (* means track was incomplete; all 3 CDs also included interviews)

CD1: Purple Haze*/I Don't Live Today*/Remember*/Stone Free*/Cherokee Mist*/Star Spangled Banner*/Bleeding Heart*/Testify Part 1*/Drivin' South*/I'm A Man*/Like A Rolling Stone*/Little One*/Red House*/Hey Joe/Instrumental*/I'm Your Hoochie Coochie Man *(sic)*/Purple Haze/Instrumental*/The Wind Cries Mary/Love Or Confusion*/Foxy Lady
CD2: Third Stone From The Sun*/Killing Floor*/Wild Thing/Tax Free*/May This Be Love*/Mr. Bad Luck/The Burning Of The Midnight Lamp*/The Burning Of The Midnight Lamp/You've Got Me Floating*/Spanish Castle Magic/Bold As Love/One Rainy Wish/Little Wing/Drivin' South/The Things I Used To Do*/All Along The Watchtower/Drifter's Escape/Cherokee Mist*/Voodoo Chile*/Voodoo Child (Slight Return)/...And The Gods Made Love*/1983...(A Merman I Should Turn To Be)*
CD3: Have You Ever Been (To Electric Ladyland)?*/Voodoo Chile*/Voodoo Chile*/Rainy Day, Dream Away*/Come On (Part 1)/Fire*/Manic Depression/Astro Man*/The Stars That Play With Laughing Sam's Dice*/Machine Gun*/Stepping Stone*/Room Full Of Mirrors/Angel/Rainy Day Shuffle*/Valleys Of Neptune*/Drifting*/Send My Love To Linda/Send My Love To Linda*/South Saturn Delta*/God Save The Queen*/Dolly Dagger/Can I Whisper In Your Ear*/Night Bird Flying/Getting My Heart Back Together Again*

OVER LABOR DAY WEEKEND IN 1988, THE US RADIO SYNDICATION NETWORK Westwood One made available for broadcast an afternoon-long special entitled *Jimi Hendrix: Live And Unreleased*. It comprised a four-hour (with commercials) documentary of Jimi's life and career, and a further hour devoted to the broadcast of the Experience's L.A. Forum concert from April 26, 1969. The special was intended, so the Hendrix Estate hinted, as a preview of a radio series that would be devoted to rare Hendrix recordings, though this never materialised.

To distant British fans, the entire exercise was frustratingly tantalising – the prospect of hours of unissued Hendrix material being weighed against the US-only airing of Westwood One's product. The release of this three-CD set brought everyone back down to earth. With the commercials stripped away, the documentary section of the show now stretched for a little over three hours. Meanwhile, the L.A. Forum show wasn't licensed for official UK release.

Worse still, the format of the show was designed to appeal to American audiences, not British. If the BBC had broadcast a similar epic, they would no doubt have aired a succession of rare recordings, introducing each one with relevant information and then leaving the music to be heard without interruptions. In the States, the unissued tracks were stitched into a music/words tapestry that often meant that collectors were reduced to straining their ears to catch a few seconds of previously unheard guitar wizardry beneath the banal narration.

Interviews with Pete Townshend, Mick Jagger, Mitch Mitchell, Chas Chandler and Hendrix himself accompanied the music, creating a show that was highly enjoyable once, but quickly palled thereafter. A large proportion of the musical content was less "Live And Unreleased" than over-familiar, and almost all of the unreleased tracks were presented in incomplete, sometimes fragmentary form.

That said, the set did offer the first legal exposure to gems like Jimi's solo demos of 'Angel', 'Voodoo Child (Slight Return)' and 'Cherokee Mist'; the jazzy, experimental textures of the instrumental 'South Saturn Delta', from June 1968; a wonderful 1967 studio take of 'Look Over Yonder', preceding the *Rainbow Bridge* cut by a year; and a radical remix of '1983' from *Electric Ladyland*. Also included, though, was Sting performing 'Little Wing' (legal problems forced Castle to withdraw the set because Sting hadn't given his permission) and several Little Richard tracks which didn't actually feature Hendrix at all.

The CD booklet, the back cover and the actual encoding of the CDs themselves all gave different information about the number of tracks on each disc. Large segments of the show were grouped together as one 'track', making it impossible to cue up a particular performance on any of the CDs. Equally annoying were the many errors in the skimpy booklet, which claimed, for example, that Jimi worked with Curtis Knight in 1964, not 1965/66.

Are You Experienced/ Band Of Gypsys/ Hendrix In The West/ War Heroes

Polydor 839 875-2 (UK), 1989

TRACKS: As original CDs

THIS POINTLESS BOX SET COLLECTED A SEEMINGLY RANDOM SELECTION OF Hendrix LPs, in their most primitive state of CD remastering, and added a skimpy booklet.

THE JIMI HENDRIX REFERENCE SERIES

Fuzz, Feedback & Wah-Wah

Hal Leonard HL00660036 (USA), 1989

TRACKS (ALL EXTRACTS): Drivin' South/Drivin' South/Freedom/Peace In Mississippi/Purple Haze/Manic Depression/Love Or Confusion/Bold As Love/Spanish Castle Magic/Spanish Castle Magic/If Six Was Nine/Little Miss Lover/Stone Free/Foxy Lady/Foxy Lady/Third Stone From The Sun/EXP/Wild Thing/Look Over Yonder/Ezy Ryder/Red House/Stone Free/Are You Experienced?/The Burning Of The Midnight Lamp/Up From The Skies/Up From The Skies/Little Miss Lover/Voodoo Child (Slight Return)/Still Raining, Still Dreaming/Belly Button Window/Tax Free/Changes/Who Knows/Are You Experienced?/Straight Ahead/In From The Storm/Red House/Red House/Red House/Message To Love/Tax Free/1983...(A Merman I Should Turn To Be)

Whammy Bar & Finger Grease

Hal Leonard HL00660038 (USA), 1989
Repackaged as HL00660279 in 1992

TRACKS (ALL EXTRACTS): Star Spangled Banner/Third Stone From The Sun/Machine Gun/Star Spangled Banner/Pali Gap/Look Over Yonder/I Don't Live Today/Tax Free/Cherokee Mist/Star Spangled Banner/Machine Gun/Machine Gun/Ain't No Telling/Machine Gun/Machine Gun/House Burning Down/Hey Joe/Red House/Foxy Lady/Astro Man/Drivin' South/Machine Gun/Spanish Castle Magic/Manic Depression/Bold As Love/Third Stone From The Sun/Third Stone From The Sun/Astro Man/Drivin' South/Machine Gun/God Save The Queen/Spanish Castle Magic/Machine Gun/The Wind Cries Mary/May This Be Love/Third Stone From The Sun/Astro Man/Star Spangled Banner/Spanish Castle Magic

Red House:
Variations On A Theme

Hal Leonard HL00660040 (USA), 1989
Repackaged in 1992 as HL00699358

TRACKS: Six versions of Red House by Hendrix, plus Red House by John Lee Hooker.

Octavia & Univibe

Hal Leonard HL00660275 (USA), 1993

TRACKS (ALL EXTRACTS): Purple Haze/Fire/One Rainy Wish/Little Miss Lover/Tax Free/MLK/Angel/Little Wing/Dolly Dagger/Pali Gap/Star Spangled Banner/Night Bird Flying/Drifting/Astro Man/Instrumental Solo/In From The Storm/Star Spangled Banner/Dolly Dagger/Machine Gun/Little Wing/Machine Gun/Midnight/Voodoo Child (Slight Return)/Hey Baby (The Land Of The New Rising Sun)/Who Knows

Rhythm

Hal Leonard HL00660281 (USA), 1993

TRACKS (ALL EXTRACTS): Killing Floor/Killing Floor/Stone Free/Stone Free/Manic Depression/Love Or Confusion/Love Or Confusion/Wait Until Tomorrow/Ain't No Telling/Fire/Drivin' South/You've Got Me Floating/Bold As Love/Little Wing/Little Wing/Castles Made Of Sand/Electric Lady Land/Voodoo Child (Slight Return)/Jam 292/Still Raining, Still Dreaming/Come On (Part 1)/Stone Free/Freedom/Johnny B. Goode/Jam H290/Gypsy Eyes/Message To Love/Message To Love/Lover Man/Bleeding Heart/Beginning/Midnight/Spanish Castle Magic

THESE INSTRUCTIONAL PACKAGES COMPRISED 'THE JIMI HENDRIX REFERENCE Series', a combination of music and transcription whose aim, according to Alan Douglas, was "rooting Jimi in the academic arena, and analysing every aspect of the guitar defined by Jimi Hendrix". With the exception of the *Red House* volume, the 'Reference Series' (originally intended to run to 12 volumes) was aimed at sight-reading guitar players rather than casual listeners. The CDs or cassettes in each package were fully annotated on music sheets, together with explanations of how, to quote the project consultant Laurence Juber, Jimi "unlocked the potential of noise for music-making by learning how to control its power by subtle techniques".

All five CDs contained otherwise unavailable material, but all but one of them – *Red House* the exception again – divided Jimi's work into fragments illustrating a particular technique or trademark. Approached without scholarly intentions, the CDs formed strange collages of sound, offering frustratingly brief extracts from solos and riffs, like a 'name that tune' quiz without a question-master. "It's specifically intended for musicians and would-be musicians," Douglas told ICE magazine. "It's an inspiration process; you hear Hendrix do these things, and if you make an attempt to get where he gets, hopefully you'll find something of your own along the way."

Fuzz, Feedback & Wah-Wah and *Rhythm* covered self-explanatory ground, but *Whammy Bar & Fingergrease* probably needs further explication: 'whammy bar' is the name given to the guitar's vibrato (tremolo) arm, which stretches the string and alters its pitch; 'finger grease' is a catch-all description for Jimi's unique approach to the instrument. Amusingly, this CD included one brief performance ('God Save The Queen') which wasn't by Jimi but by a sound-alike. 'Octavia & Univibe' were electronic devices that Hendrix utilised during the second half of his recording career. The Octavia was a Roger Mayer invention, which doubled the note that Jimi was playing, at the same pitch but an octave higher; while the Univibe, a device first used at Woodstock, produced a quavering guitar sound similar to that you'd obtain if you played the instrument through a Leslie speaker.

For the non-musician, the most enticing of these five CDs was *Red House: Variations On A Theme*. Originally, this was meant to feature eight complete renditions of Jimi's blues classic, but restrictions of space limited the contents to six, plus a redundant, coals-to-Newcastle cover by R&B veteran John Lee Hooker, which should have been replaced by one of Jimi's original studio takes of the song.

The six performances on the CD were as follows: Winterland, October 10, 1968; TTG Studios, October 29, 1968; Royal Albert Hall, February 24, 1969; LA Forum, April 26, 1969; Berkeley, May 30, 1970; and Randall's Island, July 17, 1970 (listed here as coming from the Newport Pop Festival, June 20, 1969).

According to *Guitar Player* editor Tom Wheeler, "It's a collection that demonstrates that if Jimi Hendrix had confined himself solely to conventional blues structures and ignored the other realms in which he was so creative, so dominant, he still could have established himself as one of the electric guitar's towering practitioners." A similar theory later inspired the :Blues CD, which proved easier to enjoy.

Cornerstones 1967-1970

Polydor 847 231-2 (UK), October 1990

TRACKS: Hey Joe/Purple Haze/The Wind Cries Mary/Foxy Lady/Crosstown Traffic/All Along The Watchtower/Voodoo Child (Slight Return)/Have You Ever Been To (Electric Ladyland)?/Star Spangled Banner/Stepping Stone/Room Full Of Mirrors/Ezy Ryder/Freedom/Drifting/In From The Storm/Angel/Fire/Stone Free

THIS RATHER POINTLESS TV-ADVERTISED COMPILATION WAS ASSEMBLED BY UK Polydor to capitalise on the hype around the 20th anniversary of Jimi's death. Besides the early singles, its choice of material was strange, and the decision to end the set with two previously unissued tracks, 'Fire' and 'Stone Free' from Atlanta, on July 4, 1970, provoked some cynicism – particularly when neither of them was included on the *Stages* box set, which included a less-than-full CD devoted to this show. *Cornerstones* was soon withdrawn and replaced by *The Ultimate Experience*.

Sadly, the packaging was as sloppy as fans had come to expect from UK-originated projects – photos printed back to front, erroneous information, etc. Particularly baffling was the notion that Jimi and Billy Cox had first performed together "while they were in the army in 1981"…

Lifelines

Reprise 9 26435-2 (USA), November 1990

TRACKS (* means track is incomplete; CDs 1-3 also include interviews):

CD1: Purple Haze*/I Don't Live Today*/Remember*/Stone Free*/Cherokee Mist*/Star Spangled Banner*/Bleeding Heart*/Testify Part 1*/Drivin' South*/I'm A Man*/Like A Rolling Stone*/51st Anniversary*/Little One*/Red House/Hey Joe/Instrumental*/I'm Your Hoochie Coochie Man *(sic)*/Purple Haze/Instrumental*/The Wind Cries Mary/Love Or Confusion*/Foxy Lady
CD2: Are You Experienced?*/Third Stone From The Sun*/Killing Floor*/Wild Thing*/Rock Me, Baby*/Tax Free*/May This Be Love*/Mr. Bad Luck/The Burning Of The Midnight Lamp*/The Burning Of The Midnight Lamp/You've Got Me Floating*/Spanish Castle Magic/Bold As Love/One Rainy Wish*/Little Wing*/Little Wing/Drivin' South/The Things I Used To Do*/Can You Please Crawl Out Your Window*/All Along The Watchtower/All Along The Watchtower*/Like A Rolling Stone*/Drifter's Escape/Cherokee

Mist*/Voodoo Chile*/Voodoo Child (Slight Return)/... And The Gods Made Love*/1983...(A Merman I Should Turn To Be)

CD3: Have You Ever Been (To Electric Ladyland)?*/Voodoo Chile*/Rainy Day, Dream Away*/Come On (Part 1)/Fire*/Manic Depression/Astro Man*/The Stars That Play With Laughing Sam's Dice*/Machine Gun*/Stepping Stone*/Room Full Of Mirrors/Angel/Rainy Day Shuffle*/Valleys Of Neptune*/Drifting*/Send My Love To Linda/Send My Love To Linda*/South Saturn Delta*/God Save The Queen*/Dolly Dagger/Can I Whisper In Your Ear*/Night Bird Flying/Getting My Heart Back Together Again*

CD4: Tax Free/Red House/Spanish Castle Magic/Star Spangled Banner/Purple Haze/I Don't Live Today/Voodoo Child (Slight Return)/Sunshine Of Your Love

THE *LIVE AND UNRELEASED* SET UNVEILED IN BRITAIN DURING 1989 WASN'T issued in the States. Instead, an expanded version appeared in America a year later. It fundamentally repeated the contents of the UK edition, merely tinkering a little with the track listing and, wherever possible, upgrading the sound quality of the rare recordings. "We found better sources for some of the tracks we used on the original radio show," explained engineer Bruce Gary, "and upgraded them accordingly for this new set. We found a stereo version of 'Angel', we've expanded the 'Red House' track from the Paris concert, and we have a better version of the '1983' demo track."

Lifelines won more kudos from fans for restoring the April 26, 1969 L.A. Forum show that had filled the final hour of the original Westwood One radio special in 1988. Sadly, though, this CD didn't contain the entire performance, as Gary attempted to explain: "'Foxy Lady' just didn't fit timewise on the CD, and since it's already available on the *Jimi Hendrix Concerts* package, we decided to omit it." At least some logic was in evidence, unlike the decision to mix out some of Hendrix's vocals on the L.A. performance of 'Voodoo Child (Slight Return)'.

Sessions

Polydor 847 232-2 (UK), February 1991

COMPRISES US CDs OF: *Are You Experienced/Axis: Bold As Love/Electric Ladyland/The Cry Of Love*

THE BOX ITSELF WAS ATTRACTIVE ENOUGH, BUT OTHERWISE THIS FOUR-CD SET was simply repackaging and unnecessary repackaging at that. Included were the revamped US versions of the first four Hendrix studio albums. Accompanying the box was a brief, rather ugly booklet, with surreal sleeve-notes by John Tracy. This was how he described *Electric Ladyland* charting in America: "beneath the Star Spangled Banner 6307 galloped into her equivalent tabulations ... precious yellow metal was claimed on November 19th". Congratulations if you realised that was the date when the album qualified for a gold disc.

The Ultimate Experience

Polydor 517 235-2 (UK), November 1992

TRACKS: All Along The Watchtower/Purple Haze/Hey Joe/The Wind Cries Mary/Angel/Voodoo Child (Slight Return)/Foxy Lady/The Burning Of The Midnight Lamp/Highway Chile/Crosstown Traffic/Castles Made Of Sand/Long Hot Summer Night/Red House/Manic Depression/Gypsy Eyes/Little Wing/Fire/Wait Until Tomorrow/Star Spangled Banner/Wild Thing

THE ULTIMATE EXPERIENCE WAS APPARENTLY COMPILED BY UK POLYDOR VIA market research, asking the public what songs they'd like to hear Jimi play, so it was surprising not to find 'My Way' or 'Bohemian Rhapsody' in the track listing. And I'd like to meet the fans who determined that the lacklustre (by Jimi's standards) 'Wait Until Tomorrow' belonged in this company.

Otherwise, this was a reasonably sensible selection, made up entirely of studio recordings until the final double-whammy of 'Star Spangled Banner' (Woodstock, of course) and 'Wild Thing' (auto-destruction at Monterey). 'Red House' was the version from the US *Smash Hits* LP, not Jimi's choice from his first UK album (Alan Douglas repeated the same decision when he prepared *Are You Experienced* for 1993 release.)

When the Hendrix Estate's engineer, Joe Gastwirt, heard this album, he was apparently appalled by its poor sound quality, based as it was on second- or third-generation tapes, so he remastered it via HDCD technology, and this revamp was made available in 1993, tagged as a 'Special Edition' with slightly different packaging.

Calling Long Distance

Univibes UV-1001 (Ireland), November 1992

TRACKS: The Burning Of The Midnight Lamp/Little Miss Lover/Foxy Lady/Catfish Blues/Oh Man, Is This Me Or What (interview)/Purple Haze/Fire/Getting My Heart Back Together Again/Spanish Castle Magic/Slow Walkin' Talk/Instrumental Improvisation/Hey Baby (The Land Of The New Rising Sun)/Red House

LONGTIME HENDRIX ARCHIVIST CAESAR GLEBBEEK WAS THE PRIME MOVER behind the excellent Hendrix fanzine *Univibes*, one of two (the other being *Jimpress*) European magazines that were a boon to collectors in the Nineties.

Teetering on the brink of official recognition from the Estate during the final years of the Alan Douglas era, *Univibes* pulled off a triple coup – exclusive rights to market, for subscribers only, otherwise unreleased Jimi Hendrix recordings. In each case, the contents of *Calling Long Distance*, *EXP Over Sweden* and *Jimi In Denmark* fell below the rigorous checks on sound quality which Douglas would have imposed on an official CD release. But *Univibes* subscribers certainly weren't complaining.

Calling Long Distance was scheduled to coincide with what would have been Jimi's 50th birthday. Immaculately packaged, with copious notes and rare photos, it was presented in strict chronological order. It opened with one of the first live performances of 'The Burning Of The Midnight Lamp', from Sweden in September 1967, then returned to Britain a month later for an alternate take of 'Little Miss Lover' – complete with additional wah-wah, wolf-whistles and authentic acetate crackles.

'Foxy Lady' and 'Catfish Blues' came from the Dutch TV show *Hoepla*, in November 1967; the latter in particular was a brilliant performance, with a swaggering vocal and an ebullient Mitch Mitchell drum solo. An amusing interview from December 1967 was the only non-musical track, before a Canadian 'Purple Haze' from March 1968, with the customary waves of feedback introducing the song. 'Fire' and 'Getting My Heart Back Together' were taken from the Experience's set at the Miami Pop Festival in May 1968, while 'Spanish Castle Magic', from the Winterland residency of October that year, was previously available in edited form on the *Whammy Bar* and *Finger Grease* instructional CD.

Perhaps the most intriguing track on the album was 'Slow Walking Talk', a song by Soft Machine member Robert Wyatt, taped during Jimi's October 1968 studio sessions in Hollywood. Jimi performed bass on this jazzy cut, having apparently heard Wyatt run through the song only once. The two minutes of 'Instrumental Improvisation' from summer 1970 were self-explanatory: Billy Cox and Hendrix, investigating the melodic potential of a theme that was never completed. *Calling Long Distance* came to an end with two tracks from one of Jimi's last gigs, in Copenhagen the week after the Isle of Wight festival. 'Hey Baby (New Rising Sun)' opened with an elegiac overture; the song was almost incidental to this beautiful performance, which faded out as the band slid into 'All Along The Watchtower', and where else to end but with 'Red House', adding another ten minutes of majestic blues guitar to the Hendrix catalogue.

The Experience Collection

MCA MCAD4-10936 (USA), September 1993

As PART OF THEIR 'FINAL' REVAMPING OF THE ORIGINAL HENDRIX STUDIO albums, MCA issued this four-CD box set, which included the remastered and repackaged editions of *Are You Experienced*, *Axis: Bold As Love* and *Electric Ladyland*, alongside the 'definitive' compilation, *The Ultimate Experience*. It was a brilliant idea, except for the fact that almost every track already featured on one or other of the three studio records.

Live Forever

Guts & Grace 521321-2 (USA), 1993

TRACKS FEATURING HENDRIX: Message To Love/Fire/I Don't Live Today

LATIN GUITAR HERO CARLOS SANTANA LAUNCHED HIS OWN RECORD LABEL, Guts & Grace, with a record that featured live recordings taken from the final concert tours by legendary artists. This was either a heartfelt tribute or a macabre obsession. In Jimi Hendrix's case, it yielded three previously unreleased tracks from his shows at the Berkeley Community Theater on May 30, 1970.

Santana was allowed to take 'Message To Love' and 'Fire' from the first show, and 'I Don't Live Today' from the second. Also included on *Live Forever* were songs by Marvin Gaye ('Joy' and 'What's Going On'), Bob Marley ('Natural Mystic' and 'Exodus'), Stevie Ray Vaughan ('Riviera Paradise') and John Coltrane ('Ogunde').

:Blues

Polydor 521 037-2 (UK), April 1994
Revised edition MCA 111 060-2 (UK), November 1998

TRACKS: Getting My Heart Back Together Again/Born Under A Bad Sign/Red House/Catfish Blues/Voodoo Chile/Mannish Boy/Once I Had A Woman/Bleeding Heart/Jam 292/Red House/Getting My Heart Back Together Again

WHEN British author Charles Shaar Murray wrote *Crosstown Traffic* in the late Eighties, one of his avowed intentions was to stress that Jimi Hendrix owed as much, if not more, to the black music tradition than to white rock'n'roll. Unbeknown to Murray, his views were echoed by Eighties/early Nineties Hendrix Estate curator Alan Douglas. According to archivist and Knack drummer Bruce Gary, "Alan Douglas has been trying to put together a proper Hendrix blues album since 1974. He went to the archives back then and listened to a lot of material. But he was working on so many projects that it fell by the wayside." In 1992, Douglas confirmed: "We've got an unreleased studio blues album that's going to blow everybody's mind".

Two years later *:Blues* (yes, that colon was part of the title) emerged as the first major collection of unheard Hendrix studio cuts since *Nine To The Universe*. During those 14 years, countless hours of out-takes had been made available on unofficial bootleg releases, demonstrating that the fans wanted to hear more: with *:Blues*, they finally got it. Not that rarity was the sole rationale behind the release. Douglas set out to expose Jimi's roots in black music, from the acoustic blues of the inter-war period to the uptown R&B that co-existed alongside the early Experience releases in the Sixties.

The familiar delta picking of 'Hear My Train A Comin', first released on the *Soundtrack Recordings From The Film Jimi Hendrix* LP in 1973, evidenced Jimi's little-seen command of the acoustic idiom, while 'Red House' satisfied the demand for Fifties-style urban blues. 'Catfish Blues' (as first heard on the *Univibes* CD, *Calling Long Distance*) showed Jimi moving Chicago blues into the acid-rock era, while 'Hear My Train A-Comin' (the same cut used on *Rainbow Bridge*) remains the pinnacle of Hendrix's extemporised blues soloing. The unissued tracks filled in some of the detail, and in one case opened up new territory. 'Born Under A Bad Sign' was an Albert King R&B hit from 1967, a magnificent blending of Fifties blues and Sixties Southern soul. With the Band Of Gypsys two years later, Hendrix explored the theme, never quite dominating it – this instrumental rendition rambled somewhat – but striking enough moments of inspiration to make the journey worthwhile in its own right.

'Voodoo Chile Blues' followed 'Catfish Blues', the vintage song from which it drew its inspiration. 'Voodoo' was an earlier take from the session which produced the lengthiest cut on *Electric Ladyland*; Hendrix dragged UFO signals from his guitar while Mitch Mitchell, Steve Winwood and Jack Casady vamped behind him. In theory, Muddy Waters' macho anthem, 'Mannish Boy', was an ideal selection for a Hendrix blues record. But this rendition, begun in April 1969 and overdubbed the following January, was less a document of Jimi's love for Chicago blues than of his inability to transform it into the funk idiom. It shuffled along without a hint of emotional involvement or even technical grace as compensation.

'Once I Had A Woman' was a long – perhaps over-long – alternative to the track issued on *Midnight Lightning*. Jimi's guitar work was fluid enough, but the band abandoned the blues structure several minutes into their jam, without ever finding a more fruitful direction. Not so with the perennial 'Bleeding Heart', familiar from live tapes, but presented here in a studio rendition from May 1969.

'Jelly 292' came from the same session as 'Jam 292', on the *Loose Ends* album. "It was Alan's title," explained Bruce Gary, "something to distinguish between the tracks. You got jam and you got jelly." Suitably enough, the song was little more than a Fifties-style novelty instrumental, souped up for the psychedelic age. 'Electric Church Red House' was the grand title for a rendition of Jimi's blues anthem previously issued on the instructional CD, *Variations On A Theme*. Unlike most of his extended takes on the song, this was a studio version, cut in October 1968, which rolls gracefully on the back of Hendrix's guitar, and dissolves in a howl of feedback. From there, Douglas cued up that *Rainbow Bridge* live classic from Berkeley in 1970, ending an excellent album on a majestic note.

The original 1994 release of *:Blues* supervised by Alan Douglas included an epic feat of annotation by Michael J. Fairchild, plus a selection of tiny photographs. Surprisingly, when Experience Hendrix took over Jimi's catalogue, they didn't delete Douglas's creation, as they did with everything else he'd assembled; but they did revamp it. The music was left unchanged, but a new and much shorter essay was commissioned from Jeff Hannusch, accompanied by correspondingly larger photos. The recording date for 'Bleeding Heart' was corrected, Douglas' engineer, Mark Linett, lost his credit, but Douglas and Bruce Gary did get to keep their names in the small print, albeit virtually buried atop a tinted photograph.

Experience Hendrix

CD1 only: Telstar TTVCD 2930 (UK), September 1997
Ltd edition 2-CD reissue: MCA 112 383-2 (UK), September 2000
Reissue, CD1 only: MCA MCD 11671 (UK), April 2002

TRACKS: CD1: Purple Haze/Fire/The Wind Cries Mary/Hey Joe/All Along The Watchtower/Stone Free/Crosstown Traffic/Manic Depression/Little Wing/If Six Was Nine/Foxy Lady/Bold As Love/Castles Made Of Sand/Red House/Voodoo Child (Slight Return)/Freedom/Night Bird Flying/Angel/Dolly Dagger/Star Spangled Banner
CD2: Highway Chile/Gloria/It's Too Bad/Spanish Castle Magic/Hear My Train A-Comin'/Lover Man/I Don't Live Today/Purple Haze

To CELEBRATE THE LAUNCH OF THE NEW REGIME CONTROLLING JIMI'S ESTATE, Experience Hendrix prepared an eponymous compilation. A sensible collection of studio cuts plus the Woodstock rendition of the US national anthem, it was briefly joined in 2000 by a second CD, featuring eight tracks from the new *Jimi Hendrix Experience* box set. By 2002, normal service was resumed, albeit with different artwork to the original Telstar release.

Voodoo Child:

The Jimi Hendrix Collection

Universal 170-322-2 (UK), July 2002

TRACKS
CD1 (STUDIO): Purple Haze/Hey Joe/The Wind Cries Mary/Fire/Highway Chile/Are You Experienced?/The Burning Of The Midnight Lamp/Little Wing/All Along The Watchtower/Crosstown Traffic/Voodoo Child (Slight Return)/Spanish Castle Magic/Stone Free/Izabella/Stepping Stone/ Angel/Dolly Dagger/Hey Baby (New Rising Sun)/Third Stone From The Sun
CD2 (LIVE): Fire/Hey Joe/I Don't Live Today/Hear My Train A-Comin'/Foxy Lady/Machine Gun/Johnny B. Goode/Red House/Freedom/Purple Haze/Star Spangled Banner/Wild Thing

THE LATEST IN A LONG SERIES OF 'DEFINITIVE' HENDRIX COMPILATIONS, *Voodoo Child* was a less obvious selection than it first appeared. Five years after *Experience Hendrix*, Janie Hendrix and John McDermott elected to subvert the greatest hits concept by slipping a handful of alternate takes and less familiar recordings among the hit singles and key album tracks.

Three songs were borrowed from the *Jimi Hendrix Experience* rarities box set: the full-length stereo master of 'Highway Chile'; the pre-Albert Hall rehearsal of 'Spanish Castle Magic' from February 1969; and the April 1969 remake of 'Stone Free'. 'All Along The Watchtower' wasn't the single mix, but the earlier Chas Chandler production unveiled on *South Saturn Delta*. Most useful of all was the decision to revert to the original single mixes of 'Stepping Stone' and 'Izabella', prepared by the Band Of Gypsys in January 1970, as opposed to the overdubbed versions completed later that year (and heard on *The First Rays Of The New Rising Sun*). Of the two, 'Stepping Stone' displayed the most spectacular differences, with Buddy Miles' drums pounding double-time through the opening phrases, way higher in the mix than on any of the other versions of the song.

A bonus disc of live material was offered as a 'limited edition', though every copy seemed to include it. Its contents were pulled from the previous 30 years of Hendrix archive releases, covering everything from Monterey in 1967 through Winterland in 1968 to the Isle of Wight two years later. All three of those sources were listed as 'previously unavailable', as the Monterey and Winterland sets had been deleted and the Isle of Wight had yet to be reissued at this point. Otherwise the only rarity was 'Foxy Lady' from Maui in July 1970, a cut strangely missing from the wanna-be 'official' release of the Maui shows, *The Rainbow Bridge Concerts*, a few months later.

Martin Scorsese Presents The Blues: Jimi Hendrix

MCA B0000698-02 (US), September 2003

TRACKS: Red House/Voodoo Chile/Come On (Let The Good Times Roll)/Georgia Blues/Country Blues/Hear My Train A-Comin'/It's Too Bad/My Friend/Blue Window/Midnight Lightning

IN 2003, *THE BLUES* WASN'T JUST A GENRE OR EVEN A LIFETIME'S CALLING, but a multi-media marketing exercise. It was even trademarked, which presumably means that you can't sing about having the blues this morning without paying someone a royalty. Under the supervision of legendary film director Martin Scorsese, Universal Music Enterprises, Sony Music, PBS and Harper Collins joined forces to produce a seven-part TV series, a DVD set, soundtrack CDs, a *Best Of The Blues* collection, a five-CD epic titled *The Blues – A Musical Journey*, a book of the same title, and twelve individual-artist CDs by acts as diverse as Robert Johnson, Keb' Mo' and, indeed, Jimi Hendrix.

Like the 1994 album *:Blues*, the Scorsese collection (actually compiled by the Experience Hendrix team) was faced with the less than arduous task of highlighting Jimi's roots in the blues. Jimi's old friend Lithofayne 'Fayne' Pidgeon contributed a touching personal memoir to the same effect.

The current Hendrix catalogue was the source for all but two tracks, with the compilers opting for such reliable favourites as 'Voodoo Chile' from *Electric Ladyland* and the live-in-the-studio 'Hear My Train A-Comin'' from the *Jimi Hendrix Experience* box set. The two additions to the canon were each intriguing, in their own way. 'Blue Window' came from the March 1969 sessions that Hendrix produced for the Buddy Miles Express, out of which came the *Electric Church* album. On this occasion, Hendrix joined the horn band in the studio, for a performance that sounded closer to the output of Miles' previous band, The Electric Flag.

'Georgia Blues' was something else again: the first appearance in the official Hendrix catalogue by that unwitting bane of Jimi collectors, Lonnie Youngblood. Not that this track came from the endlessly regurgitated studio jams they shared at the birth of Hendrix's recording career. No, for reasons unexplained, Hendrix joined Youngblood's band at the Record Plant in March 1969, adding some uncharacteristically orthodox blues guitar behind Lonnie's rather delicious lead vocals and saxophone. The same track had appeared with a different mix as 'Mother Mother' on the *Two Great Experiences* CD earlier in the year; but this time around, Hendrix was given the composing credit, not Youngblood.

CD SINGLES

The Singles Collection

MCA 0602498145036 (Europe), 2003

TRACKS

CD1: Hey Joe/Stone Free

CD2: Purple Haze/51st Anniversary

CD3: The Wind Cries Mary/Highway Chile

CD4: The Burning Of The Midnight Lamp/The Stars That Play With Laughing Sam's Dice

CD5: Foxy Lady/Manic Depression

CD6: Crosstown Traffic/Gypsy Eyes

CD7: Voodoo Child (Slight Return)/Hey Joe/All Along The Watchtower

CD8: Stepping Stone/Izabella

CD9: Dolly Dagger/Night Bird Flying

CD10: Auld Lang Syne/Silent Night/Little Drummer Boy/Three Little Bears

---

YES, IT WAS REPACKAGING, BUT BEAUTIFUL REPACKAGING: A SET OF SINGLES in facsimile sleeves offering period European artwork. 'Voodoo Child' repeated the package that topped the UK charts in the wake of Jimi's death; while 'Dolly Dagger' offered a first commercial release to the promo single issued to coincide with the *First Rays* album in 1997.

Most important was the musical contents, as 'Stepping Stone' and 'Izabella' were the long-lost Band Of Gypsys versions, issued briefly as a single in 1970 but then overdubbed by Mitch Mitchell for subsequent reissues. This set also transferred the original mono mixes of 'Purple Haze', 'The Wind Cries Mary' and 'The Burning Of The Midnight Lamp' onto CD for the first time. And there was an elegant booklet featuring a nostalgic essay by Hendrix expert Steve Rodham plus photos of more rare 45s.

All Along The Watchtower

Polydor 879 583-2 (France), 1991

TRACKS: All Along The Watchtower/Star Spangled Banner/Come On (Part 1)

A MARGINALLY ALTERNATE TAKE OF 'COME ON (PART 1)' WAS THE PRIME selling point of this single.

All Along The Watchtower

Polydor PZCD 100 (UK), October 1990

TRACKS: All Along The Watchtower/Voodoo Child (Slight Return)/Hey Joe/Crosstown Traffic

FOUR FAMILIAR EXPERIENCE RECORDINGS, COINCIDING WITH THE RELEASE of *Cornerstones*.

Are You Experienced?

MCA 155-635-2 (Europe), 1999

TRACKS: Are You Experienced?/Remember/Highway Chile

THREE TRACKS FROM THE DEFINITIVE RELEASE OF JIMI'S DEBUT ALBUM, ISSUED two years after the appearance of the full CD.

Crosstown Traffic

Polydor PZCD 71 (UK), April 1990

TRACKS: Crosstown Traffic/Voodoo Child (Slight Return)/All Along The Watchtower/Have You Ever Been (To Electric Ladyland)?

TO CASH IN ON THE SELECTION OF 'CROSSTOWN TRAFFIC' AS THE SOUNDTRACK to a Wrangler jeans commercial, Polydor issued this *Electric Ladyland* track as an A-side. The Estate even put together a wonderful life-in-the-New-York-streets video to match. Interestingly, the songs here are listed as being taken from "the forthcoming CD, *Wild Thing: The Best Of Jimi Hendrix*," a project that was immediately cancelled when the Estate got to hear about it.

Day Tripper

Rykodisc RCD 31-008 (USA), 1988

TRACKS: Drivin' South/Getting My Heart Back Together Again/Day Tripper

RYKODISC (OR PERHAPS WE SHOULD BLAME ALAN DOUGLAS) INFURIATED collectors by issuing Radio One, and then releasing alternate takes of the first two songs listed above on this CD single, which wasn't issued in Britain. These were claimed to be un-broadcast out-takes, but they were actually the versions aired in 1967.

Dolly Dagger

MCA MCD 11636 (Europe), 1997

TRACKS: Dolly Dagger/Night Bird Flying/Astro Man

A SAMPLER FOR THE (SUPPOSEDLY) DEFINITIVE *THE FIRST RAYS OF THE NEW Rising Sun* compilation of Hendrix's latter-day studio recordings.

Gloria

Polydor 887 585-2 (Germany), 1988

TRACKS: Gloria/Hey Joe/Voodoo Child (Slight Return)/Purple Haze

THE FAMILIAR 1968 STUDIO JAM THROUGH VAN MORRISON'S SONG, PLUS three Experience studio favourites.

Gloria

Polydor 859 715-2 (Australia), 1994

TRACKS: Gloria/Stone Free/51st Anniversary/The Stars That Play With Laughing Sam's Dice

'GLORIA' was joined here by one hit single and two early B-sides.

Hey Joe

Polydor 879 083-2 (UK), 1993

TRACKS: Hey Joe/Stone Free/51st Anniversary/Can You See Me?

THE FRUITS OF the first few Experience recording sessions in 1966.

Merry Christmas And Happy New Year

MCA 088-155-651-2 (USA), November 1999

TRACKS: Little Drummer Boy/Silent Night/Auld Lang Syne (medley)/Three Little Bears

BAGGY'S STUDIOS IN NEW YORK (SEE *THE BAGGY'S REHEARSAL SESSIONS*) WAS the venue for this impromptu Band of Gypsys jam through seasonal favourites – originally distributed in the Seventies as a promotional single. With Millennium Eve nearing, Experience Hendrix dug out the tape, and combined it with the equally playful Experience out-take, 'Three Little Bears', as originally aired on *War Heroes* in 1972.

The Peel Sessions

Strange Fruit SFPSCD 065 (UK), December 1988

TRACKS: Radio One/Day Tripper/Wait Until Tomorrow/Hear My Train A-Comin'/Spanish Castle Magic

PREDATING THE *RADIO ONE* ALBUM BY SEVERAL MONTHS, THIS CD EP FEATURED the entire broadcast contents of the Experience's last BBC Radio session on December 15, 1967. These tracks were originally aired on *Top Gear*, as presented by John Peel and Tommy Vance – hence the title and this set's inclusion in a long series of Strange Fruit releases. Shame about the tedious generic artwork, though.

Purple Haze

Polydor PZCD 33 (UK), January 1989

TRACKS: Purple Haze/51st Anniversary/All Along The Watchtower/Hey Joe.

THREE EXPERIENCE A-sides, plus the slightly more obscure '51st Anniversary'.

The Wind Cries Mary

Polydor 863 917-2 (UK), November 1992

TRACKS: The Wind Cries Mary/Fire/Foxy Lady/May This Be Love

FOUR STUDIO tracks, issued to promote *The Ultimate Experience*.

SECTION 3

UNOFFICIAL CDS

IN ONE SENSE, ALMOST ALL OF THE CDS REVIEWED IN THIS BOOK HAVE BEEN 'unofficial', in the sense that Jimi Hendrix never sanctioned their release. But this section is reserved for albums that were not OK'd by Jimi, his executors, or the various controllers of the Estate, but which have – by some legal loophole or another – still managed to reach the commercial marketplace.

With very few exceptions, these records were/are worthless. Historically, they could have boasted some minor pretension to significance if (a) they were properly annotated, (b) they were compiled with some sense of their place in Jimi's career, (c) they were cheap and (d) they weren't so infuriatingly repetitious. But few escaped at least one of these pitfalls, and most fell for them all.

Releases qualify for this 'unofficial' tag for one or more of the following reasons: (1) They contain recordings that would never have been approved for release, or reissue, by Jimi Hendrix. (Of course, it could be said that this also applies to most of the legal, 'official' CDs issued since his death.) (2) They feature tracks whose ownership has become impossible to ascertain, and which have effectively (if not legally) fallen into the public domain (i.e. anyone can release them without the risk of being sued for breach of copyright). (3) They are made up of official releases by Jimi, which have passed out of copyright in the country where they are being reissued. This applies in particular to Japanese CDs made up of pre-1969 Hendrix studio recordings. (4) They contain officially unreleased live recordings, which were briefly legal somewhere in the world thanks to the complete breakdown of international copyright co-operation in the late Eighties and early Nineties. In almost all cases, it would have been ruled illegal to sell these releases (mostly from Germany and Italy) in the UK, had anyone been bothered to bring a lengthy, protracted and expensive lawsuit to prove the point. (5) They are an offshoot of the ongoing legal dispute between Experience Hendrix and the successors of Mike Jeffery's late 60s management company, Yameta Productions (see Disputed Territory below).

In the world of bootlegs, the mere fact that a record is 'unofficial' (and therefore often illegal) can make the heart of the diehard fan beat a little faster. Sadly, the Hendrix catalogue proves that unofficial and exciting aren't synonyms. There are plenty of unreleased Hendrix gems available on 100% bootleg releases, but those can't and won't be offered for sale in respectable record stores. For the most part, the 'unofficial' recordings included on these CDs are the dregs of Jimi's career, thrown onto the marketplace with only one aim in mind: to part fools from their money.

Four groups of 'unofficial' recordings crop up time and time again on these albums. After decades of shoddy and frequently misleading releases, more or less definitive representations of three of these sets of sessions have been released in the past decade. The fourth, the 1968 Scene Club jam, sounds shambolic whichever way you slice it, so the only relevant factor here is price. If you really have to sample this material – and only the Royal Albert Hall concert from February 1969 is recommended to anyone but completists – then the albums singled out below are where you should turn. The 'Avoid At All Costs' listing that follows this section rounds up all the other dubious contenders for your cash.

Disputed Territory

TO MOST PEOPLE'S EYES, THERE IS NO POSSIBLE DISPUTE OVER THE OWNERSHIP of the Jimi Hendrix catalogue. After his death in 1970, his legacy was left to his Estate, which was controlled by Jimi's manager Mike Jeffery until his own mysterious death in 1973. Then Jimi's friend Alan Douglas assumed control, until he was ousted in the mid-Nineties, and the family-run Experience Hendrix company took over.

But in the early years of the new century, Mike Jeffery has made a strange return from the dead – in the form of the inheritors of Yameta, the management company to which he signed Jimi Hendrix in the Sixties. The Mike Jeffery Estate has now begun to license Hendrix material to the British label Purple Haze Records, who have released a series of archivally interesting but legally (how can I put it?) 'indecisive' packages. Experience Hendrix have exerted legal pressure to have some of these releases removed from mainstream outlets in the UK; but others, such as (at the time of writing) the *Astro Man* box set, have remained on open sale. In March 2004, Purple Haze turned the tables, launching a lawsuit to force Experience Hendrix to delete the official *Axis: Bold As Love* CD, on the grounds that Jeffery's Estate actually own the rights. The dispute will no doubt end up in the courts, somewhere in the world, before too long. But until then, the (in the eyes of the Hendrix Estate) 'offending' releases have been listed below.

Also included in this section are unauthorised reissues of officially released Hendrix material; interview albums (though be warned: these are constantly repackaged in a variety of guises); and a handful of other oddities that, at various times, have cropped up on the shelves of the world's megastores.

Astro Man

Alchemy JHBX 1 (UK), 2003

AT THE TIME OF GOING TO PRESS, THIS GLORIOUSLY UNOFFICIAL – AT LEAST AS FAR as the Hendrix Estate were concerned – six-CD box set was freely available in mainstream retail outlets and on world-renowned websites. The set was copyrighted to the Mike Jeffery Estate, and exemplified the problems facing Experience Hendrix while the legal dispute between the two sides boiled towards a climax.

All six of these albums were also being issued by various outlets individually, either on vinyl or CD. Together, they contained three concert recordings: Paris 1968 (as found on the long-deleted official set, *Stages*); and both Stockholm shows from 9 January 1969. The remaining CDs featured studio out-takes unheard on official releases, from a succession of takes of 'Red House' and 'I Don't Live Today' from the first album sessions, to a plethora of in-the-studio jams from 1970, notably an amazing romp through and beyond the title track. Much of the material offered only minor variations on Experience Hendrix releases, but collectors were still tantalised by this set's riches. How long it will be freely available remains to be seen.

Axis Outtakes

Purple Haze HAZE002 (UK), 2003

LEGALITIES ASIDE, THE TITLE OF THIS TWO-CD SET WAS LESS THAN ACCURATE, as just eight of its 21 tracks came from the making of Hendrix's second album. Several songs here were taken from official releases, notably 'Little Wing' (alias 'Angel') and 'Somewhere'. Others were crude manipulations of the master tapes to produce apparently alternate takes ('Spanish Castle Magic' was a prime offender). But the more intriguing offerings included 'South Saturn Delta' before the horn overdubs; an early take of 'Bold As Love', and 'Takin' Care Of No Business' with the legendary tuba overdub.

Many tracks suffered from appalling sound quality, however, while others, like the apparently endless 'Jazz Jimi Jazz' jam, were unlistenable for musical reasons. Ironically, the clearest reproduction of all was reserved for 'Cherokee Mist' – which was actually a Hendrix imitator performing a Jimi-inspired take on 'God Save The Queen'.

Band Of Gypsys

On Stage CD 12022 (Italy), 1993

A LIAS THE OFFICIAL *BAND OF GYPSYS* CD, PRESENTED IN A DIFFERENT ORDER, with cheapskate packaging. The complications of European Community law in the early Nineties allowed this set to appear at budget price across the Continent, and then be imported into Britain as a 'legitimate' release.

Best Of Artist Selection

Jasrec JECD 1030 (Japan), 1993

S TUNNING TITLE, EQUALLY IMPRESSIVE ARTWORK, WHICH DIDN'T BOTHER TO illustrate Jimi or anything relating to him. This was a batch of original Experience studio recordings, presented in less than perfect quality.

Big Artist Selection

Pigeon GX-448 (Japan), 1993

W HY DID THE COVER SHOW A CAR, A STREET-SIGN AND A CLOCK? MAYBE JIMI was meant to turn up for a photo session, but overslept. You would too, if you had to plough through another entirely random selection of Experience studio tracks.

Cafe Au Go Go
Jam Session

Koine K880802 (Italy), February 1989

O NLY THE MOST LENIENT OF COPYRIGHT LAWS – AS FOUND IN LATE EIGHTIES' Italy – would have allowed the 'legal' release of this album, documenting a lacklustre jam session at New York's Cafe Au Go Go in March 1968, within a week or two of the infamous Scene Club jam. Amusing to hear once, but that's all.

Collection

Graffiti GRCD 13 (Switzerland), August 1990

NOT SO MUCH A *COLLECTION* AS A DOCUMENT OF JIMI'S SHOW AT THE L.A. Forum in April 1969. The entire set, minus 'Foxy Lady', appeared on the official US box, *Lifelines*. 'Foxy Lady' duly appeared here, but in return 'Tax Free' didn't. And they wonder why people prefer bootlegs...

Crosstown Conversation

Tabak CBAK 4082 (UK), June 1994

ONE OF SEVERAL CDs FEATURING EXTRACTS FROM AN EARLY 1970 INTERVIEW featuring the original Experience trio, who were announcing a reunion that never happened. *Jimi Hendrix 1970* featured a longer version of the encounter.

Fire

The Entertainers CD 297 (Italy), 1993

"LIVE PERFORMANCES" WAS WHAT THE COVER OF THIS CHEAPO-CHEAPO effort promised, and what it delivered as well – all borrowed from the official *Live At Winterland* release, except for 'Little Wing' and 'Lover Man', which came from *Hendrix In The West*. Sound quality here was vastly inferior to the legitimate releases.

Gold Collection

Digital Deja 2 D2CD03 (Italy), 1992

ITS ORIGINS WERE HIGHLY DUBIOUS, AS FAR AS UK COPYRIGHT LAW WAS concerned, but the contents were intriguing, mixing live material from Stockholm 1967 (*Stages*), the BBC (*BBC Sessions*), Holland 1967 (*Calling Long Distance*), Stockholm 1969 (*Stockholm Concert 69*) and the L.A. Forum (*Collection*).

Golden Best

Lily NLC-64 (Japan), 1993

THE JAPANESE RECORD BUSINESS AT ITS MOST ENVIRONMENTALLY CONSCIOUS, recycling the Experience's first few months in the studio without wasting a morsel of brain power or imagination. The cover showed a branch of the Hard Rock Café.

Great Hits U.S.A.

Jasrec GH-1841 (Japan), 1993

THE EARLY EXPERIENCE STUDIO SIDES, ONE MORE TIME – RECORDED IN ENGLAND, despite the title.

Hendrix Speaks

Rhino R2 70771 (USA), October 1990

HERE'S 45 MINUTES OF INTERVIEWS, TAPED IN LONDON IN DECEMBER 1967, and in California in June 1969.

Hey Joe

Legend WZ 90025 (Germany), 1994

THE COVER PHOTO SHOWING HENDRIX AS A RIGHT-HANDED GUITARIST didn't inspire confidence, but the contents were an interesting, if hardly definitive, collection of 1966-1970 studio recordings, in not quite perfect quality.

The Interview

CID Productions CID 006 (UK)

THE COMPLETE MEATBALL FULTON INTERVIEW FROM DECEMBER 1967 (as sampled on Hendrix Speaks).

The Interview

CD Card CCD 4082 (UK), 1994

CROSSTOWN CONVERSATION, UNDER A DIFFERENT TITLE.

Introspective

Baktabak CINT 5005 (UK), April 1991

CROSSTOWN CONVERSATION AGAIN, 'SPICED' WITH EXCERPTS FROM THE SCENE Club jam.

Introspective/
The Wind Cries Mary

Baktabak CINT 25006 (UK), 1993

AS ABOVE, PLUS AN OFFICIAL POLYDOR CD SINGLE.

Jimi Hendrix Experience

Rockstars In Concert 6127092 (Holland), 1992

LIVE RECORDINGS PURLOINED FROM THE OFFICIAL MONTEREY, STOCKHOLM (*Stages*) and Paris (*Stages* again) releases, plus three songs from Stockholm 1969 (*Stockholm Concert 69*).

Jimi Hendrix 1967: Standing Next To A Mountain

If 6 Was 9 JH01 (Sweden), c. 1991

SWEDISH INTERVIEWS FROM 1967, PACKAGED IN A LIMITED EDITION (1,000 copies) imitation tape box with two glossy photos.

Jimi Hendrix 1970

Discussion MERMAN 1983 (UK), 1991

A FULL 65 MINUTES OF THE EXPERIENCE REUNION INTERVIEW.

Los Angeles Forum

Burning Airlines PILOT 200 (UK), 2004

OFFICIALLY UNAVAILABLE SINCE THE DELETION OF THE LIFELINES BOX SET, this gig made an unscheduled reappearance without the intervention of the Hendrix Estate. On a bonus CD, Burning Airlines included an audience tape of Jimi's final gig, at the Fehmarn festival in Germany.

Live At Monterey Pop Festival

ITM Media 960008 (Italy), 1993

A S ALSO HEARD ON AN OFFICIAL CD, WHICH WAS CHEAPER, SOUNDED BETTER, and featured the songs in the right order.

No More A Rolling Stone

Purple Haze REDR001CD (UK), 2004

TAKING ADVANTAGE OF THEIR COMMERCIAL UNAVAILABILITY, PURPLE HAZE slipped the Monterey and Stockholm gigs from 1967 back into print on this 2-CD set.

Purple Haze

On Stage CD 12010 (Italy), 1993

THE JIMI HENDRIX EXPERIENCE RELEASE LISTED ABOVE, ON THE ROCKSTARS In Concert label, with minor variations of track listing.

Purple Haze

Jasrec EX-3012 (Japan), 1993

ORIGINAL EXPERIENCE RECORDINGS IN THE 127TH (GUESS) PERMUTATION achieved by the Japanese. Marvellously irrelevant cover artwork, too.

Purple Haze
In Woodstock

ITM Media 960004 (Italy), April 1993

UNTIL 1999, THIS NOW IRRELEVANT RELEASE WAS THE ONLY PLACE (bar an out-and-out bootleg) to find several officially unissued tracks from the Woodstock set. Shame they got the date of the festival wrong, and chose a cover photo from the Isle of Wight instead of Woodstock.

The Rainbow Bridge Concert

Purple Haze HAZE001 (UK), 2002

THIS CLAIMED TO OFFER HENDRIX'S TWO JULY 1970 MAUI CONCERTS IN FULL, as filmed for the *Rainbow Bridge* movie. In fact, both recordings were incomplete: 'Spanish Castle Magic' should have opened the set, and 'Stone Free' to close it. Also, the sound quality was dreadful throughout, which was particularly disappointing given the remarkable performance Hendrix gave during the first show. The second set seemed to run slightly slow, simply adding to the chaos.

Red House

The Entertainers CD 294 (Italy), 1992

EIGHT TRACKS LIFTED FROM *ELECTRIC LADYLAND*, PLUS TWO FROM HENDRIX *In The West*, all in appalling sound quality. One track is listed as 'Woodoo Child'.

Special Collection

Jasrec GRN-52 (Japan), 1993

THE JAPANESE *PURPLE HAZE* COMPILATION, IN 'SPECIAL' DISGUISE.

Stockholm Concert 69

Purple Haze HAZE 003 (UK), 2004

TWO SHOWS FROM JANUARY 9, 1969, DELIVERED IN REMARKABLY FINE quality, and never issued in full on any official release.

Super Selection

Echo EVC 336 (Japan), 1994

ECHO'S TRACK COMPILER CAME UP WITH HIS CHOICE OF HENDRIX STUDIO recordings. His wife ran her eyes down the list, and cried out, "Super selection, darling". But why did the front cover picture a Beverly Hills T-shirt?

The Very Best Of Jimi Hendrix

Millenium MILCD 03 (Italy), 1994

NOT EXACTLY THE VERY BEST, BUT THERE HAVE BEEN WORSE ALBUMS THAN this purporting to offer Hendrix's finest moments. This repeated the second disc of *The Gold Collection* set.

The Lonnie Youngblood Sessions

WITHOUT EVER ACHIEVING A HIT RECORD IN HIS OWN RIGHT, SAXOPHONIST and singer Lonnie Youngblood has sold more albums than many more famous performers. Not that he could, or probably would, take much pride in this fact. Aside from his diehard fans in the mid-Sixties, scarcely a handful of the tens of thousands of people who've purchased Youngblood's 1965 recordings with Jimi Hendrix could have had the slightest interest in Lonnie or his music.

For both men, it was just another set of sessions. Youngblood was hustling for a hit single, at a time when the R&B and pop markets were susceptible to anyone who could hit a two-minute groove and make it stick on the dance floor. Hendrix, meanwhile, was scuffling gig to gig and session to session. He doubtless made the most of his touring pedigree, when he'd played back-up behind stars like Jackie Wilson, Little Richard and Sam Cooke in the Southern states. Impressed by his reputation and flair, Youngblood taped nine tunes with a small R&B band, allowing Hendrix to cut loose with an occasional solo, but mostly restricting him to rhythm work. 'Go Go Place' and 'Go Go Shoes' appeared as a Youngblood single on Fairmount in 1966 (dated 1963 on the label to avoid contractual complications). Early in 1967, a second 45 appeared, coupling 'Soul Food' with 'Goodbye Bessie Mae'.

Meanwhile, several other Hendrix/Youngblood tracks were overdubbed by (relatively) obscure vocalists and issued on singles. 'She's A Fox' was released by The Icemen on Samar in 1966, and the same label was also responsible for Billy LaMont's version of 'Sweet Thang'. 'That Little Old Groove Maker' appeared as the flipside of Jimmy Norman's 'You're Only Hurting Yourself' on 20th Century Fox as late as 1968. The remaining Youngblood/Hendrix tracks were instrumentals titled 'Under The Table' and 'Wipe The Sweat', each of which survived in several different versions.

Within months of Lonnie's death, Maple Records in New York compiled a Youngblood/Hendrix album called *Two Great Experiences Together*. Most of its tracks were overdubbed with sound-alike lead guitar to make them sound more like Hendrix. A year later, *Rare Hendrix* repeated much of this material, but added tracks that had no Hendrix involvement. The same scam has been pulled countless times since, with 'fake' Hendrix recordings usually outnumbering the authentic ones. So raise a small glass to Youngblood for his hand in releasing the album below, which shone a more or less honest light on the whole escapade.

Two Great Experiences

BMG 82876 51686 2 (Germany), May 2003

TRACKS: Mother, Mother/Under The Table (Take 1)/Under The Table (Take 2)/Wipe The Sweat (Take 1)/Wipe The Sweat (Take 2)/Wipe The Sweat (Take 3)/Go Go Shoes/Go Go Place/Soul Food/Goodbye Bessie Mae/Sweet Thing/Groove Maker (Take 1)/Groove Maker (Take 2)/She's A Fox/Go Go Shoes (single version)/Go Go Place (single version)/Soul Food (single version)/Goodbye Bessie Mae (single version)

" **NEVER THOUGHT I'D SEE THE DAY WHEN THESE SONGS WOULD COME BACK OUT,"** Lonnie Youngblood admitted in the liner notes to this long overdue album. "The tapes were stolen out of New York's Abtone Studio and sold to companies that have since earned millions of dollars. When I looked up, the tapes were all over the place. People have robbed me blind. I never got any of the money."

Sadly, the release of this album attracted far less attention than many of the scurrilous cash-ins released in the Seevnties. Decades of cash-ins and rip-offs ensured that the potential audience for this release was minimal. But at least this set included music that Hendrix would have recognised as his own, even if he never would have wanted anyone else to hear it.

Included here were both sides of the two vintage Lonnie Youngblood singles, plus 13 variations on the tracks that Hendrix originally recorded. 'She's A Fox' was the original Icemen single, while 'Groove Maker (Take 2)' and 'Sweet Thing' were alternate versions of the 45s by Jimmy Norman and Billy LaMont respectively. The rest was a mix of backing tracks and stereo remixes, a couple of which – listed as takes 2 and 3 'Wipe The Sweat' – retained some of the mock-Hendrix guitar licks added after Jimi's death. And the music? Club soul circa 1965: simple R&B grooves, with flickering guitar licks, and sub-Stax vocals.

None of which explained the presence of the opening track, explained away in the liner notes as another 1965 recording, but actually taped in 1969 at the Record Plant in New York. A different mix of the same rather enjoyable blues jam was included on the official *Martin Scorsese Presents The Blues* album a few months after this release.

The Curtis Knight Sessions

IN THE IMMEDIATE AFTERMATH OF JIMI'S DEATH, BY FAR THE MOST PROLIFIC sources of 'unofficial' Hendrix releases were his two stints of recording with another would-be R&B star of the mid-Sixties, Curtis Knight. Using the pseudonym Jimmy James, Hendrix was a member of his band sporadically between October 1965 and May 1966, but during that time he helped Knight record around a dozen studio tracks, and was also taped on stage at two, possibly more, East Coast club shows.

On October 15, 1965, in fact, Jimi signed an exclusive recording deal with Knight's recording boss, Ed Chalpin of PPX Records. This came back to haunt him after he found fame in England, when PPX pressed Track/Polydor for legal recompense for Hendrix's alleged breach of contract. Jimi did nothing to calm the legal waters by naïvely agreeing to return to PPX in July/August 1967 and take part in further Curtis Knight sessions, during which a further 12 tracks were taped.

Knight issued two singles from the PPX recordings around the start of 1966. Then, after the success of 'Hey Joe' and 'Purple Haze', many singles and albums based on the Knight/Hendrix recordings were prepared for release. When Jimi died, the live tapes of the duo in action were also thrown onto the market in equally haphazard fashion. In both instances, studio trickery was something used to alter the sound and presentation of the material. Some but not all of these problems were solved by the 'definitive' series collected on the box set reviewed below.

The Complete PPX
Studio Recordings

SPV 088-29802 (Germany), 2000

GENERATIONS OF HENDRIX FANS HAD BEEN BURNED BY ALBUMS CLAIMING that the Curtis Knight recordings revealed Jimi's "eternal fire" or "genius". But by the end of the century, there was room in all but the hardest hearts for an anthology that would place this formative, if erratic, material in its proper context. It required honesty and diligence, two qualities not often apparent in the music business. The returns would be modest, to say the least, but there would be the reward of knowing that an open sore in Hendrix's musical legacy had finally been healed.

So the arrival in 1996 of the first of a series entitled *The Authentic PPX Studio Recordings* was greeted with some enthusiasm by collectors – until they viewed the contents. What they wanted was a definitive presentation of the Hendrix sessions; what they got was a jumbled and frequently misleading set of CDs that presented as many questions as they answered. They were sold as "approved original recordings from the musical Estate of Jimi Hendrix", though the legal Estate of Jimi Hendrix certainly hadn't approved them.

However these German albums still offered the most comprehensive selection of the troubled Hendrix/Knight collaborations.

In 2000, all six were repackaged in a low-budget box set, which was available at double-CD price if you shopped around. There were only two problems with the title of *The Complete PPX Studio Recordings*: the contents were far from complete, and half the material was recorded not in the studio but on stage. Among the titles previously released on vinyl but never transferred to CD were: 'No Such Animal Parts 1 & 2' (a 1965 jam issued as a single in 1971), the unedited 1967 studio versions of 'Get That Feeling' and the 'Day Tripper-Future Trip-Flashing' medley', and a full album's worth of live tracks, including 'Bo Diddley', 'Have Mercy', 'Hang On Sloopy', 'Hold On To What You've Got', 'Just A Little Bit', 'Land Of 1000 Dances', 'Let's Go, Let's Go, Let's Go', 'One Night', 'Something You've Got', 'Stand By Me', 'Twist And Shout', 'Walkin' The Dog', 'Wooly Bully' and 'You Got What It Takes'. That doesn't even begin to take in the tangled legacy of alternate takes and different edits: that way madness lies.

And talking of madness: there is still a theoretical void for another trawl through the Knight tapes, which would present a definitive collection of what Hendrix actually recorded in 1965 and 1967, without any of the subsequent overdubs and studio meddling. But it's hard to imagine one ever having the stomach for the task – or, indeed, the marketing ability to make it a commercial proposition.

The Authentic PPX
Studio Recordings
Vol. 1: Get That Feeling

TRACKS: Get That Feeling/How Would You Feel?/Hush Now/No Business/ Simon Says/Gotta Have A New Dress/Strange Things/Welcome Home

IN THEORY, THIS COLLECTION DUPLICATED THE TRACK LISTING OF *GET THAT FEELING*, the first Curtis Knight/Jimi Hendrix album issued by US Capitol in 1967. In practice, there were several major differences: the title track was edited down from ten minutes to five, 'Hush Now' ran substantially longer than it had done three decades earlier, and several cuts were artificially extended by careful tape trickery.

Such modifications suggest sleight of hand, but *Get That Feeling* was more than a magician's con-trick. In 'How Would You Feel?', blatantly inspired by Bob Dylan's 'Like A Rolling Stone', it boasted arguably the first black protest single of the rock era. While borrowing the ascending chord sequence, chiming guitar fills and trademark organ of Dylan's tune, it added strident political anger, via both its lyrical jibes at racism and poverty, and the grizzled edginess of Hendrix's fuzz guitar. Equally striking was 'Strange Things', a Bo Diddley-inspired garage-rock performance of genuine eeriness. The remaining 1965 cuts were more playful, with Jimi adding chunky rhythm chords and spiky fills to formulaic R&B dance tunes with obvious commercial pretensions, if not potential.

The trio of 1967 performances was more erratic. Jimi played wah-wah on the rambling jam, 'Hush Now', and fuzz bass on the remaining cuts. 'No Business' stirred another distant Dylan comparison with its bluesy humour, but the title track was altogether more substantial – both as a piece of James Brown funk and as a vehicle for Hendrix's subterranean bass rumbling.

The Authentic PPX Studio Recordings

Vol. 2: Flashing

TRACKS: Love, Love/Day Tripper/Gloomy Monday/Fool For Your Baby/Don't Accuse Me/Hornet's Nest/Flashing/Oddball/Happy Birthday

ONCE AGAIN, A LATE SIXTIES CAPITOL LP WAS THE BLUEPRINT FOR THIS ALBUM and again, careful study revealed the differences between this 'Flashing' and its 1968 counterpart. A more important divide separated the surprisingly ambitious studio outings from 1965, and the more formless jams from summer 1967. Of the latter 'Day Tripper', 'Flashing', and 'Oddball' featured Hendrix on fuzz bass, more restrained by his inexperience with the instrument than inspired by its sonic potential. Curtis Knight overdubbed vocals onto both 'Love Love' and 'Happy Birthday' after Jimi had left the studio, without enlivening the guitarist's fidgeting with his effects pedal. Only 'Gloomy Monday' revealed any genuine Hendrix spirit, though the mix was so chaotic that it was impossible to distinguish him from the efforts of a second guitarist added after the event.

Three 1965 recordings were more rewarding – even the slightest of them, 'Don't Accuse Me', a Ray Charles/Bobby Bland cross with a thin but stinging Hendrix solo. 'Fool For Your Baby' betrayed the influence of the British Invasion – imagine a 'supergroup' comprised of The Animals and The Zombies – with some delicate guitar work worthy of the future creator of 'Little Wing'. And then there was 'Hornet's Nest', a 1965 Curtis Knight single that was a fractious blend of organ, fuzz guitar and manic drums, all set to a 'Nut Rocker'-style riff. Like 'How Would You Feel?' and 'Strange Things' from the previous volume, it countered many of the insults hurled at the Hendrix/Knight recordings over the previous 30 years.

The Authentic PPX Studio Recordings

Vol. 3: Ballad Of Jimi

TRACKS: UFO/You Don't Want Me (instrumental)/Better Times

Ahead/Future Trip/Wah Wah (instrumental) [Hush Now]/Everybody Knew But Me/Mercy Lady Day (instrumental) [Love, Love]/If You Gonna Make A Fool Of Somebody/My Best Friend (instrumental) [The Ballad Of Jimi]/The Ballad Of Jimi/Second Time Around (instrumental) [Get That Feeling]

NO SOONER HAD HENDRIX BEEN BURIED IN 1970 THAN CURTIS KNIGHT announced the 'discovery' of a chilling recording on which he seemed to prophecy his own death. 'The Ballad Of Jimi', so Knight said, had been recorded some three years earlier, but featured such insightful lyrics as "though Jimi's gone, he's not around, his memory lingers on", and "he's not gone, he's just dead". While Knight intoned these spine-tingling messages, there was Jimi messing with his wah-wah in the background, apparently unmoved by his impending doom.

Well, only part of that story was true. The track was recorded in 1967, but the vocals – surprise, surprise – were redubbed in autumn 1970 to cash in on Jimi's demise. Knight's tall story did nothing to boost the credibility of either himself or his Hendrix recordings – and neither, to be honest, did this compilation. Besides that appalling fake 'tribute', *Ballad Of Jimi* featured a ragbag of formless jams from 1967, most of which were featured on the first two volumes of this series in more appealing form. Then there was a quartet of 1965 demos, two of which ('Better Times Ahead' and 'If You Gonna Make A Fool Of Somebody') had no discernable Hendrix input whatsoever. That probably was Jimi's guitar on 'UFO' and 'Everybody Knew But Me', but as his hero Bob Dylan would have said, there was nothing, really nothing to turn off.

The Authentic PPX Studio Recordings

Vol. 4: Live At George's Club

TRACKS: Drivin' South (instrumental)/Ain't That Peculiar/I'll Be Doggone/I've Got A Sweet Little Angel/Bright Lights, Big City/Get Out Of My Life, Woman/Last Night (instrumental)/Sugar Pie Honey Pie [I Can't Help Myself]/What'd I Say/Shotgun

FOR A GENERATION OF INNOCENTS, THEIR INITIAL EXPOSURE TO THE GENIUS OF Jimi Hendrix came from the carelessly packaged budget albums that littered the record racks in the early Seventies, recycling the same sorry archive of Curtis Knight live recordings.

Removed from that sense of exploitative disappointment, these tapes of the Knight/Hendrix ensemble had their moments – not least the opening cut, the familiar revamp of an Albert Collins R&B instrumental that remained in Jimi's live repertoire until the end of 1967. His lead vocal on Lee Dorsey's 'Get Out Of My Life, Woman' was another pleasant distraction from Knight's functional performances of bar band standards, while 'I've Got A Sweet Little Angel' took him at least halfway towards the focused blues power of 'Red House'. But the rest, which included a studio cut ('Last Night') overdubbed with fake applause, was mediocre, at best.

For years, all of these live recordings were credited as having been taped at St. George's Club, Hackensack, New Jersey, on Boxing Day 1965. Indeed, Knight opened this album by introducing "Jimmy James" on "25 plus 1". But as ever with the Knight tapes, the facts were less straightforward, as there may well have been as many as three different sources for this material, and some of Knight's dialogue may have been added when the tapes were being exhumed in the Seventies. What wasn't faked, however, was Jimi's voice, heard engaging in conversation at the start of 'Drivin' South', and later introducing 'What'd I Say'.

The Authentic PPX Studio Recordings

Vol. 5: Something On Your Mind

TRACKS: California Night/Level (instrumental) [Hush Now]/I Feel Good/Left Alone [Bleeding Heart]/Knock Yourself Out/Something On Your Mind/I Should've Quit You [Killing Floor]/Hard Night (instrumental)/I'm A Man/Instrumental [Oddball]

BACK TO THE BARS, AND THE EDITING DESK: THIS WAS ANOTHER BIZARRE concoction of live and studio recordings, the latter including an artifically elongated version of 'Hush Now', an undubbed, vocal-free mix of 'Oddball', and the surprisingly funky 'Knock Yourself Out' from 1965. More impressive were some of the concert tapes, with Hendrix taking lead vocals on 'I'm A Man', 'California Night' and an over-excitable 'Killing Floor'. Of them all, 'California Night' was the keeper, not for its blues cliches, but for Jimi's expressive singing, answered by fluent licks from his guitar. Only a year separated this recording from the flourishing of the Experience, and on this performance, it showed.

The Authentic PPX
Studio Recordings

Vol. 6: On The Killing Floor

TRACKS: On The Killing Floor/Money/Nobody Loves Me [California Night]/Love (instrumental) [Love, Love]/You Got Me Running [Baby What You Want Me To Do]/Mr. Pitiful/Torture Me Honey (instrumental) [Hush Now]/Sleepy Fate (instrumental) [No Business]/Satisfaction

'TORTURE ME HONEY' WAS AN APT SONG TITLE ON AN ALBUM THAT ENCAPSULATED the pitfalls of this series. Three 1967 studio tracks heard elsewhere in marginally different form were reprised here under new titles; another, 'Killing Floor', was treated to overdubbed applause. The rest was genuine club fare, from the choice of material ('Money' and 'Baby What You Want Me To Do' were in every garage-band's repertoire in 1965) to the perfunctory performances. So there were only two facets of this album to quicken the pulse: another rendition of 'California Night', featuring a Hendrix vocal, and an early example of his humour. "We're British", Knight claimed as he introduced The Rolling Stones' 'Satisfaction'. "West British", Hendrix added.

The Scene Club Jam

EARLY MARCH 1968, AND JIMI'S ON STAGE, AS USUAL. TONIGHT THE VENUE IS the Scene Club on West 46th Street, in the heart of Manhattan, where proprietor and (appropriately enough) scene-maker Steve Paul has gathered a cast of luminaries for an early-hours jam session. Alongside Jimi are members of The McCoys, the Scene's house band — yep, the same McCoys who graced us with 'Hang On Sloopy' three years earlier.

Though Jimi's just merely jamming, he's running a tape machine off the primitive mixing desk. If he knew that the scarcely coherent results of the evening's exclusive entertainment would be released again and again and again, twenty years after his death, he'd have pushed the 'off' switch fast. Instead, posterity has been gifted with a version of 'Red House' that epitomises grace under pressure, plus a less impressive 'Bleeding Heart', and plenty of lazy guitar interplay.

So far, so good, but among the Scene in-crowd is James Douglas Morrison, lead singer with The Doors, and on this night auditioning for a role as the biggest asshole in the universe. He's a star, so he has to crawl on stage and attract someone's attention. He bellows down the microphone, delivering a flurry of slurred expletives, and then collapses in a whisky-sodden heap, taking Jimi's mike-stand with him. Hendrix plays on, as if it's just another day on the edge of the apocalypse.

Fun to hear once, purgatory beyond that: so why has this non-event reappeared more times than the knife-maniac in *Halloween*? Answer: because its legal ownership is in dispute, as nobody wants to take responsibility for such nonsense.

Woke Up This Morning And Found Myself Dead

Planet PML 1068 (UK), 2001

TRACKS: Red House/Voices/Blues, Blues/Uranus Rock/Peoples, Peoples/ Woke Up This Morning And Found Myself Dead/Wow Eeh (Tomorrow Never Knows)/Gonna Take A Lot/Lime Lime Medley/Outside Woman Blues/Sunshine Of Your Lady

CHOSEN FOR ITS BUDGET PRICE (LESS THAN £3 IN LONDON STORES) RATHER THAN its packaging, this album epitomised the shoddy way in which the Scene jam has been presented over the years. For a start, two songs from other sources interrupted the track listing. Neither 'Voices' nor 'Gonna Take A Lot' had anything to do with Hendrix (though the latter was actually an attractive piece of Sixties soft soul). Meanwhile, the Scene material was presented in the wrong order, the recording was broken up into separate tracks rather than allowed to flow seamlessly, the track titles and writing credits were inaccurate, and the liner notes carefully made no mention of the music they were supposed to accompany. But other than that ...

The Experience
At The Albert Hall

FEBRUARY 24, 1969 AT THE ROYAL ALBERT HALL: THE OCCASION WAS THE JIMI Hendrix Experience's second live show in England since the Woburn Abbey festival the previous June (the first 'comeback' gig had been in the same prestigious concert hall, six days earlier). Priced out of the UK market by manager Mike Jeffery's demands from promoters, Hendrix had agreed to the shows because he realised that the Experience were in danger of antagonising their British support by their relative lack of activity.

Film director Joe Levine captured the show, during which the Experience were augmented during the encore by percussionist Rocky Dijon, and Dave Mason and Chris Wood from support group Mason, Capaldi, Wood and Frog, for a movie provisionally entitled *The Last Experience*. And so it proved to be – in Britain, at least – though the original Experience Hendrix/Redding/Mitchell trio survived a few months longer in the States.

The movie remains unreleased to this day, wrapped up in legal hassles, but that didn't prevent Ember Records issuing two 'soundtrack' albums in the early Seventies, *Experience* and *More Experience*. Both LPs were taken directly from the film audio track, not professionally recorded tapes, and their sound quality suffered accordingly. Since then, the same material has been issued on a dozen or more unofficial CDs, while the Hendrix Estate dipped into material from the same source as early as Hendrix In The West.

Ember set another unfortunate precedent back in 1971, when they claimed that *Experience* contained "probably the last recorded sounds of Jimi Hendrix". The same laughably incorrect statement has appeared on several 'unofficial' CDs. The Charly set listed below took its title from the lost film, and offered the most comprehensive collection to date of recordings from the Albert Hall experience.

The Last Experience

Charly SNAJ 720 CD (UK), September 2002

TRACKS
CD1: Introduction & Tune-up/Lover Man/Stone Free/Getting My Heart Back Together Again/I Don't Live Today/Red House/Foxy Lady/Sunshine Of Your Love/Bleeding Heart

CD2: Fire/Little Wing/Voodoo Child (Slight Return)/Room Full Of Mirrors/Announcement & Tune-up/Purple Haze/Wild Thing/The Star Spangled Banner & Smashing Of The Amps/Bleeding Heart (edited)/Room Full Of Mirrors (edited)/Hey Joe (soundcheck)/Hound Dog 1 (soundcheck)/Hound Dog 2 (soundcheck)/Hound Dog 3 (soundcheck)/Voodoo Child (Slight Return) (soundcheck)/Getting My Heart Back Together Again (soundcheck)

CD3: Tax Free/Fire/Getting My Heart Back Together Again/Foxy Lady/Red House/Sunshine Of Your Love/Spanish Castle Magic/The Star Spangled Banner/Purple Haze/Voodoo Child (Slight Return)

IT'S IRONIC THAT SUCH A COMPREHENSIVE SET OF ALBERT HALL RECORDINGS should be accompanied by liner notes that put the week's events into perspective, but fail to explain the origin of much of the music on this set. The first CD and most of the second was devoted to the 24 February show, in full, and in respectable sound quality. The two edited tracks were a waste of space, but the second CD continued with a set of previously unreleased soundcheck recordings taped before the show. Finally, the third CD featured the 18 February show, edited to fit onto one disc by omitting the pauses between songs, but losing none of the music. Lo-fi in the extreme, this audience tape was an aural ordeal to anyone not entirely devoted to the cause.

Not so the second show: there the ordeal was Jimi's, at least to begin with. Rarely can he ever have sounded so bored on stage, as he explained that the Experience would be "running through some of the old stuff, I guess, cos there's nothing else to do, is there?" But instead the trio opened with the unreleased 'Lover Man', before setting out on a sprawling 'Stone Free' that stretched for 12 minutes, with Hendrix soloing virtually at odds with the structure of the tune. 'Getting My Heart Back Together Again', as ever, provoked some of Jimi's most impassioned playing, before all three of the band stormed through 'I Don't Like Today' with manic intensity.

'Red House' was a strange mixture of offhand theatrics and full-bore commitment, as if Hendrix was testing the audience's willpower. The next few numbers were equally erratic, before Jimi delivered one of the finest single performances of his career: a 'Little Wing' of aching beauty. Then 'Voodoo Child' reverted to his previous mood; at one point he offered his guitar to anyone else who cared to take it, muttering, "I'm finished". 'Room Full Of Mirrors' jolted him back to life, while the rhythm section struggled to cope with the unfamiliar structure; and from there it was all jamming and chaos, with ex-members of Traffic on stage, and a way-out-of-tune 'Purple Haze' leading into the crescendo of 'Wild Thing' and a frenzied assault on his amplifiers. It was a curiously ambivalent farewell to the audience that had nurtured his career over the previous 30 months: Hendrix wouldn't appear in the UK again until the Isle of Wight another 18 months later.

AVOID AT ALL COSTS!

DOZENS OF FORGETTABLE AND SOMETIMES SCANDALOUSLY EXPLOITATIVE CDs have recycled material from one or more of the above sources over the past 20 years. Listed below are some of the main offenders: others have been omitted simply because their precise contents could not be verified. The 'fakes' listed below are generally Lonnie Youngblood recordings that do not feature Hendrix.

ABTONE SESSIONS
(Japan: Jimco, 1993)
Lonnie Youngblood sessions, plus fakes.

ALBERT HALL EXPERIENCE
(UK: Charly, 2001)
Royal Albert Hall recordings and 4 tracks from *The Jimi Hendrix Concerts* CD.

AT HIS BEST
(Germany: Planet, 2000)
Lonnie Youngblood & Scene recordings, plus fakes.

BEFORE THE EXPERIENCE
(Spain: Altaya, 1996)
Lonnie Youngblood & Scene recordings, plus fakes.

BEFORE THE EXPERIENCE
(UK: Charly, 1994)
Lonnie Youngblood & Scene recordings, plus fakes.

THE BEST & THE REST OF JIMI HENDRIX
(UK: Action Replay, 1991)
Scene recordings.

THE BEST OF JIMI HENDRIX
(Europe: KBox, 2001)
Lonnie Youngblood, Scene & Royal Albert Hall recordings, plus fakes.

BLEEDING HEART
(UK: Castle, 1994)
Scene recordings.

CHEROKEE
(Italy: Dog'n'Roll, 1993)
Lonnie Youngblood recordings, plus fakes.

COLLECTION
(Holland: Collection, 1993)
Lonnie Youngblood, Scene & Royal Albert Hall recordings, plus fakes.

THE CRAZY WORLD OF JIMI HENDRIX
(Japan: Jimco, 1994)
Lonnie Youngblood, Scene & Royal Albert Hall recordings.

DRIVIN' SOUTH
(UK: Jungle, 2000)
Curtis Knight recordings.

EARLY CLASSICS
(USA: Special Music, 1988)
Curtis Knight recordings.

EARLY DAZE
(UK: Hallmark, 1996)
Lonnie Youngblood recordings.

THE EARLY JIMI HENDRIX – LIVE
(Germany: Fortune, 1993)
Lonnie Youngblood recordings, plus fakes, all overdubbed with applause for extra listening pleasure.

THE EARLY YEARS
(UK: Charly, 1994)
Lonnie Youngblood recordings.

EXPERIENCE
(Australia: Rayon, 1990s)
Royal Albert Hall recordings.

EXPERIENCE
(Holland: Signal, 1980s)
Royal Albert Hall recordings.

EXPERIENCE
(Holland: Brilliant, 1990s)
Royal Albert Hall recordings.

EXPERIENCE
(Italy: Galaxis, 1980s)
Royal Albert Hall recordings.

EXPERIENCE
(Japan: Jimco, 1994)
Royal Albert Hall recordings

EXPERIENCE
(UK: Bulldog, 1987)
Royal Albert Hall recordings

EXPERIENCE
(UK: Nectar, 1996)
Royal Albert Hall recordings.

EXPERIENCE
(UK: Charly, 1998)
Royal Albert Hall recordings.

EXPERIENCE AT ROYAL ALBERT HALL
(Japan: Jimco, 1993)
Royal Albert Hall recordings.

EXPERIENCES
(UK: Pulsar, 1989)
Lonnie Youngblood recordings, plus fakes.

FEELING GOOD
(Holland: Music Options, 1990s)
Lonnie Youngblood & Scene recordings, plus fakes.

FEELING GOOD
(Holland: Arc, 1996)
Lonnie Youngblood & Scene recordings, plus fakes.

FIRST & LAST EXPERIENCES
(Japan: Receiver, 1996)
Lonnie Youngblood & Scene recordings, plus fakes.

THE FIRST RECORDINGS
(Japan: Overseas, 1994)
Lonnie Youngblood & Scene recordings, plus fakes.

FLASHING
(Australia: Interworld, 1994)
Curtis Knight recordings.

FREE SPIRIT
(UK: Thunderbolt, 1991)
Lonnie Youngblood recordings, plus fakes.

GANGSTER OF LOVE
(UK: Arc, 1990s)
Lonnie Youngblood recordings, plus fakes.

GOLD
(Holland: Gold, 1994)
Lonnie Youngblood, Scene & Royal Albert Hall recordings, plus fakes.

GOOD FEELING
(UK: Object, 1991)
Lonnie Youngblood & Scene recordings, plus fakes.

GOOD TIMES
(Germany: Music Reflexion, 1994)
Lonnie Youngblood & Scene recordings, plus fakes.

GOOD TIMES
(Germany: Music Mirror, 1998)
Lonnie Youngblood & Scene recordings, plus fakes.

GOOD TIMES

(New Zealand: Starburst, 1993)
Curtis Knight, Lonnie Youngblood & Scene recordings, plus fakes; and 'Down Mean Blues' & 'Monday Morning Blues' from the *Jimi Hendrix At His Best* LP series of September 1969 jam sessions.

GREATEST HITS OF JIMI HENDRIX

(Europe: Fortune, 1990s)
Lonnie Youngblood recordings, plus fakes.

THE GREAT JIMI HENDRIX

(Portugal: Goldies, 1995)
Curtis Knight & Lonnie Youngblood recordings, plus fakes.

GROOVE MAKER

(UK: Dressed To Kill, 1998)
Lonnie Youngblood & Scene recordings, plus fakes.

HENDRIX

(Holland: Royal Collection, 1991)
Lonnie Youngblood & Scene recordings, plus fakes.

HIGH, LIVE & DIRTY

(New Zealand: Music Box, 1991)
Scene recordings.

HISTORIC HENDRIX

(USA: Pair, 1995)
Curtis Knight recordings.

HOT TRIGGER

(Germany: Institute Of Art, 1994)
Lonnie Youngblood recordings, plus fakes.

HOUSE OF THE RISING SUN

(Australia: Starburst, 1993)
Curtis Knight, Lonnie Youngblood & Scene recordings, plus fakes.

IN THE BEGINNING

(Germany: Bellaphon, 1990s)
One Lonnie Youngblood recording, plus fakes.

JAMMING LIVE AT THE SCENE CLUB, N.Y.C.

(UK: Realisation, 1994)
Scene recordings.

JIMI

(Italy: Boxart, 1995)
Scene recordings.

JIMI HENDRIX

(Australia: Starburst, 1990)
Curtis Knight, Lonnie Youngblood, Scene & Royal Albert Hall recordings, plus fakes.

JIMI HENDRIX

(Germany: Bellaphon, 1994)
Polydor studio recordings of 'Hey Joe', 'Purple Haze', 'Foxy Lady', 'All Along The Watchtower', & one Lonnie Youngblood recording, plus fakes.

JIMI HENDRIX

(Holland: Everest, 1996)
Lonnie Youngblood & Scene recordings, plus fakes.

JIMI HENDRIX

(Italy: Compact, 1990)
Curtis Knight, Lonnie Youngblood & Scene recordings, plus fakes.

JIMI HENDRIX

(Italy: Cameo, 1995)
Lonnie Youngblood & Scene recordings, plus fakes.

JIMI HENDRIX

(Italy: Bella, 1997)
One Lonnie Youngblood recording, plus fakes.

JIMI HENDRIX & THE LONNIE YOUNGBLOOD BAND
(UK: Sonora, 2000)
Lonnie Youngblood & Scene recordings, plus fakes.

JIMI HENDRIX EXPERIENCE
(USA: Metro, 1990s)
Lonnie Youngblood, Scene & Royal Albert Hall recordings.

THE JIMI HENDRIX STORY
(USA: Virgin, 1997)
Curtis Knight, Lonnie Youngblood, Scene & Royal Albert Hall recordings, plus fakes.

JIMI HENDRIX: THE COLLECTION
(UK: Object, 1990)
Curtis Knight, Lonnie Youngblood & Scene recordings, plus fakes, and 'Down Mean Blues' & 'Monday Morning Blues' from the *Jimi Hendrix At His Best* LP series of September 1969 jam sessions.

KNOCK YOURSELF OUT
(UK: Jungle, 2000)
Curtis Knight recordings.

THE LAST EXPERIENCE
(Italy: Bescol, 1987)
Royal Albert Hall recordings.

THE LEGEND
(Germany: Sm'Art Art, 1995)
Polydor studio recording of 'May This Be Love', Lonnie Youngblood & Scene recordings, plus fakes.

LIVE 1968
(Europe: BMG, 1997)
Scene recordings.

LONNIE YOUNGBLOOD AND THE SO CALLED JIMI HENDRIX TAPES
(UK: Almafame, 1998)
Lonnie Youngblood & Scene recordings, plus fakes.

MASTERPIECES
(Europe: Pulsar, 1990s)
Lonnie Youngblood & Scene recordings, plus fakes.

MORE EXPERIENCE
(Japan: Jimco, 1994)
Royal Albert Hall recordings.

NEW YORK CITY 68
(USA: Red Lightning, 1990s)
Scene recordings.

NEW YORK SESSIONS
(Germany: Line, 1990s)
Scene recordings.

NIGHT LIFE
(UK: Thunderbolt, 1990)
Lonnie Youngblood & Scene recordings, plus fakes.

NYC '68
(USA: Mil, 2001)
Scene recordings.

THE PSYCHEDELIC VOODOO CHILD
(Brazil: Movie Play, 1989)
Curtis Knight & Lonnie Youngblood recordings, plus fakes.

PSYCHO
(Denmark: MCPS, 1996)
Lonnie Youngblood & Scene recordings, plus fakes.

PURPLE HAZE
(Germany: Success, 1990s)
Lonnie Youngblood, Scene & Royal Albert Hall recordings, plus fakes.

PURPLE HAZE
(New Zealand: Starburst, 1991)
Lonnie Youngblood, Scene & Royal Albert Hall recordings, plus fakes.

RARE HENDRIX
(Europe: Play, 1998)
Lonnie Youngblood recordings,
plus fakes.

RED HOUSE
(Europe: Rondo, 2000)
Polydor studio recording of 'Angel',
three BBC session recordings,
Lonnie Youngblood & Scene
recordings, plus fakes.

16 GREATEST CLASSICS
(Germany: Big Time, 1988)
Curtis Knight, Lonnie Youngblood &
Scene recordings, plus fakes.

SPOTLIGHT
(UK: Sonet, 1990s)
Royal Albert Hall recordings.

STRANGE THINGS
(Europe: Success, 1989)
Curtis Knight, Lonnie Youngblood &
Scene recordings, plus fakes; and
'Down Mean Blues' & 'Monday
Morning Blues' from the *Jimi
Hendrix At His Best* LP series of
September 1969 jam sessions.

THE SUMMER OF LOVE SESSIONS
(UK: Jungle, 2001)
Curtis Knight recordings.

SUPERSESSION
(Japan: Jimco, 1993)
Scene recordings.

TOMORROW NEVER KNOWS
(UK: Rialto, 1991)
Scene recordings.

VOICE IN THE WIND
(Holland: Trace, 1992)
Lonnie Youngblood & Scene
recordings, plus fakes.

VOICES
(Germany: Pilz, 1993)
Lonnie Youngblood recordings,
plus fakes.

VOLUME 1 & VOLUME 2
(UK: Wisepack, 1992)
Lonnie Youngblood & Scene
recordings, plus fakes.

VOODOO CHILD
(Italy: Galaxis, 1990s)
Royal Albert Hall recordings.

VOODOO GUITAR
(Europe: Trilogie, 2003)
Lonnie Youngblood & Scene
recordings, plus fakes, and an entire
CD by Little Richard featuring *none*
of his collaborations with Hendrix.

WHIPPER
(Germany: Pilz, 1994)
Lonnie Youngblood recordings,
plus fakes.

**WOKE UP THIS MORNING AND
FOUND MYSELF DEAD**
(Holland: Point, 1991)
Scene recordings.

**WOKE UP THIS MORNING AND
FOUND MYSELF DEAD**
(Holland: Start, 2000)
Scene recordings.

**WOKE UP THIS MORNING AND
FOUND MYSELF DEAD**
(UK: Red Lightning, 1986)
Scene recordings.

YOU GOT IT
(Europe: Comet, 1990s)
Lonnie Youngblood & Scene
recordings, plus fakes.

SECTION 4

GUEST APPEARANCES

Cat Mother & The All Night Newsboys:

The Street Giveth & The Street Taketh Away

LP release: Polydor 184 300 (UK), 1969
CD release: Polygram 537 616-2 (US), 1997

FROM LATE **1968** AND INTO **1969,** HENDRIX LENT HIS TALENTS AS A PRODUCER TO several artists – including this New York rock band. Included on their debut album, which was entirely produced by Jimi, was a US Top 30 hit single, 'Good Old Rock'n'Roll', which was subsequently covered with some success in the UK by the Dave Clark Five. Meanwhile, the Cat Mother album was briefly made available on CD in the late Nineties.

Eire Apparent

Sunrise

LP release: Buddah 203 021 (UK), May 1969
CD release: Sequel NEXCD 199 (UK), February 1992

TRACKS FEATURING HENDRIX: Rock'n'Roll Band/Yes, I Need Someone/The Clown/Mr. Guy Fawkes/Someone Is Sure (To Want You)/Morning Glory/Magic Carpet/Captive In The Sun/Let Me Stay

WHY DID JIMI PRODUCE AND PLAY ON ALMOST AN ENTIRE ALBUM OF MATERIAL by an otherwise unknown Irish rock band? Because they were being handled by his managers, Mike Jeffery and Chas Chandler. Hendrix contributed to their 'Rock'n'Roll Band' single and *Sunrise* album, both of which are highly enjoyable 1968 pop-rock, with some characteristically flamboyant guitar touches. Sadly, his involvement failed to boost the band's sales.

Fat Mattress

The Best Of Fat Mattress

Essential ESDCD 865 (UK), 2002

TRACK ALLEGEDLY FEATURING HENDRIX: How Can I Live?

Fat Mattress was the band that Noel Redding formed during his final months with the Experience, allowing himself to play lead guitar. During a session in August 1968, he and Mitch Mitchell cut the basic track for 'How Can I Live?' – an early version of which was featured on his posthumous solo CD, *The Experience Sessions* (see below). Hendrix was listed as producer for the session, and may also have contributed percussion to this track as it appeared on the group's eponymous debut album. Or maybe he did not.

Frank Howard & The Commanders

Old Town & Barry Soul Stirrers

Kent CDKEND 111 (UK), 1994

TRACK ALLEGEDLY FEATURING HENDRIX: I'm So Glad

A week after quitting Curtis Knight's band in summer 1966, Jimi sat in with another set of regulars at The Cheetah Club, Frank Howard & The Commanders. The attraction was no doubt the chance to work again with their bassist, his friend Billy Cox, who also wrote the band's 1966 single, 'I'm So Glad'. Cox claimed that Hendrix played rhythm guitar on the track, included 30 years later on a collection of rare Sixties R&B sides.

The Isley Brothers

The Isley Brothers: The Complete UA Recordings

EMI CDP 7-95203-2 (US), 1991

THE SLEEVE-NOTES TO THIS ALBUM SUGGEST THAT HENDRIX PROBABLY PLAYED guitar on two tracks recorded on January 14, 1964, called 'The Basement' and 'Conch'. Jimi didn't actually meet the Isleys until March 1964.

The Isley Brothers Story Volume 1: Rockin' Soul

Rhino R2 70908 (USA), 1991

TRACKS FEATURING HENDRIX: Testify Parts 1 & 2/The Last Girl/Move Over And Let Me Dance

The Story of The Isley Brothers

Epic/Legacy Z3K 65547 (USA), c. 1999

TRACKS FEATURING HENDRIX: Testify Parts 1 & 2/Move Over And Let Me Dance

THESE ISLEY/HENDRIX COLLABORATIONS ARE AUTHENTIC, HOWEVER. 'TESTIFY' WAS a double-sided single in 1964, the first release on the Isleys' own T-Neck label – and the last, at least until 1969. It's easy to see why it didn't sell: it was groundbreaking music, which came close to pioneering psychedelic soul four years too early. These were the first recordings to contain recognisable Hendrix guitar licks, and they would be noteworthy performances whether or not Jimi had played on them. Note for completists: 'Testify' exists in several subtly different mixes, found on the original 45, a late Sixties R&B compilation, and subsequent CD anthologies.

The other two songs listed above, cut during later sessions, weren't quite as thrilling as 'Testify', but they were still state-of-the-art rock-funk, 1964 style. Jimi also performed on two other Isley Brothers tracks, as yet unavailable on CD: 'Looking For A Love' and 'Have You Ever Been Disappointed?'.

King Curtis

Blues & Soul Power

Atlantic 0922-49084-2 (US), 2003

TRACK FEATURING HENDRIX: Help Me (Get The Feeling) Parts 1 & 2

IN JANUARY 1966, JIMI GUESTED WITH R&B SAXOPHONIST KING CURTIS AND his All-Stars at a recording session where they were supporting vocalist Ray Sharpe (of 'Linda Lu' fame). Split across both sides of a single, 'Help Me' was issued by Atco in 1966. Bizarrely, exactly the same backing track was then supposedly used the following year when Aretha Franklin recorded a King Curtis song, 'Save Me', for her Atlantic debut LP, and then again as the basis for Curtis' own 1969 hit single, 'Instant Groove'. But any trace of Hendrix's contribution had long since vanished in the process of overdubbing. The original track was included on an R&B anthology of Atlantic masters in 2003.

Timothy Leary

You Can Be Anyone This Time Around

LP release: Douglas 1 (USA), April 1970
CD release: Rykodisc RED 10249 (UK), May 1996

TRACK FEATURING HENDRIX: Live And Let Live

LSD GURU TIMOTHY LEARY PERSUADED JOHN LENNON TO WRITE HIM A campaign song for a planned assault on the governorship of California. Then Leary went to prison, and Lennon turned the song into a Beatles single, 'Come Together'. Also involved in the project to create Leary anthems was Jimi Hendrix, whose jam with Stephen Stills, John Sebastian and Buddy Miles – taped by Douglas purely to document the session, rather than with any particular end in mind – was overdubbed with spoken-word extracts from the would-be governor, while he was in jail. Legend has it that the song the musicians were jamming around for 25 minutes – with Jimi on bass, not guitar – was Joni Mitchell's 'Woodstock', which wasn't actually written until August 1969, three months after the apparent date of this session.

Lightnin' Rod

Doriella Du Fontaine

Restless 72663-2 (US), 1992

TRACKS FEATURING HENDRIX: Doriella Du Fontaine (Radio Edit)/Doriella Du Fontaine (instrumental)/Doriella Du Fontaine

ALAN DOUGLAS WAS PRODUCING THE PROTO-RAP GROUP THE LAST POETS IN 1969, when group member Lightnin' Rod cut this devilish piece of speech, part of a suite of 'Jail Toasts' – a clear precursor of the black music mainstream of the late Eighties and Nineties. Buddy Miles and Jimi Hendrix jammed behind him, and the track might have ruffled a few industry feathers back in 1970. But it wasn't released until 1984, by which time it was little more than an historical curio. The CD release took the basic track and subjected it to a remix and an edit.

Little Richard

The Georgia Peach

Snapper/Recall SMDCD 413 (UK), July 2002

TRACKS FEATURING HENDRIX: I Don't Know What You've Got But It's Got Me/Dancin' All Around The World

THE FULL LIST OF HENDRIX'S CAMEOS WITH LITTLE RICHARD RAN TO JUST TWO tracks (available in various different mixes and edits) and they were both featured on this budget 2-CD set. Little Richard was sporadically wonderful, Hendrix hardly audible.

Beware all albums from around the world entitled *Friends From The Beginning*, and claiming to feature an entire set of Little Richard material with Hendrix on guitar. Sadly, Jimi did not perform on any of those recordings.

Love

False Start

LP release: Blue Thumb BTS 22 (USA), December 1970
CD release: MCA MCAD 22029 (USA), 1990
CD reissue: Beat Goes On BGOCD 127 (UK), December 1993

TRACK FEATURING HENDRIX: The Everlasting First

J IMI HENDRIX AND ARTHUR LEE FIRST COLLABORATED IN EARLY 1965, WHEN LEE produced and Hendrix played on a one-off single by an artist called Rosa Lee Brooks. Sadly, the coupling of 'My Diary'/'Utee' is only available on bootleg.

In 1989, the underground market promised (but failed) to bring us an album called *The Jimi And Arthur Experience* – supposedly unveiling a lengthy session the two men may or may not have staged in March 1970. Various song titles were bandied about, but the only confirmed collaboration cut at that time was 'The Everlasting First', issued on Love's *False Start* album in late 1970, and also as a single at the same time.

Jayne Mansfield

Dyed Blonde: Marilyn Monroe & Jayne Mansfield

Snapper/Recall SMD CD 298 (UK), May 2000

TRACKS ALLEGEDLY FEATURING HENDRIX: Suey/As The Clouds Drift By

D URING HIS RESIDENCE AT ED CHALPIN'S PPX STABLE IN 1965/66, HENDRIX was invited to perform on a single by actress/pin-up Jayne Mansfield. The novelty dance time 'Suey', which featured brief flourishes of someone – possibly even Jimi – on guitar, was issued as a single. The flipside was the dreamy ballad 'As The Clouds Drift By', on which Chalpin claimed that Jimi played all the instruments. Did that include the violin section, Ed?

Buy this budget 2-CD set, and you'll get both sides of the original 45, plus an array of busty blonde bonanzas, including the appalling 'Happy Birthday Mr. President' by Ms Monroe and another dozen exercises in non-singing from Jimi's friend Jayne.

McGough & McGear/ The Scaffold

McGough & McGear

LP release: Parlophone PCS 7047 (UK), April 1968
CD release: EMI CDP 7 91877 2 (UK), 1989

TRACKS FEATURING HENDRIX: So Much/Ex Art Student

The Scaffold: The Best Of The EMI Years

CD release: EMI CDP 7 98502 2 (UK), 1992

TRACK FEATURING HENDRIX: Oh To Be A Child

MCGOUGH AND MCGEAR WERE ROGER MCGOUGH (FAMOUS LIVERPOOL poet) and Mike McCartney (brother of Paul). The Beatle connection, plus their involvement with the hit comedy/poetry/music group Scaffold, helped them get a deal for a duo album – an amusing excursion into comedy and tragedy, aided by superstar friends.

Jimi (and Noel Redding) played on three tracks during the January 1968 sessions, one of which – featuring Hendrix on toy drum – was reserved for release later that year on Scaffold's eponymous Parlophone album. Of the three, the pick was 'Ex Art Student', a fine slice of UK late-Sixties pop.

Buddy Miles Express

The Best Of Buddy Miles

Polygram 510310-2 (US), March 1997

TRACKS PRODUCED BY HENDRIX: Miss Lady/69 Freedom Special

SHORTLY AFTER THE DEMISE OF THE BAND OF GYPSYS, HENDRIX AGREED TO participate in the sessions for Buddy Miles' second album – having already penned the liner notes to his debut, *Expressway To Your Skull*. He eventually produced half of the *Electric Church* LP: the two songs listed above, plus 'Destructive Love' and 'My Chant'. During the sessions, he and the Buddy Miles Express also recorded 'Blue Window' (see *Martin Scorsese Presents The Blues*).

Noel Redding

The Experience Sessions

MCA NR 00001-2 (US), 2003

TRACKS: There Ain't Nothing Wrong/Little Miss Strange/Walking Through The Garden/She's So Fine/Little, Little Girl/How Can I Live?/Noel's Tune (Take 1)/Noel's Tune (Take 2)/Little Miss Strange/She's So Fine/Dream/Red House

ISSUED WITH ALMOST INDECENT HASTE AFTER NOEL'S UNEXPECTED DEATH IN May 2003, *The Experience Sessions* was presumably compiled with the bassist's assistance, though he might not have relished the honesty of Andy Aledort's liner notes. "Over the years, Noel remained a greatly misunderstood individual", he wrote, "in truth, Noel did little to rectify this situation." Aledort also referred to Redding's "difficult, confrontational relationship" with Hendrix, and his "great bitterness" about the financial fall-out from the Experience.

Yet *The Experience Sessions* still stood as a celebration of Redding's talent, albeit strictly under Hendrix's shadow. Noel wasn't more than a serviceable vocalist, but his songwriting showed signs of individuality, which is why Hendrix allowed him to contribute 'She's So Fine' and 'Little Miss Strange' to *Axis: Bold As Love* and *Electric Ladyland* respectively. Both tracks featured here twice, with the released versions joined by out-takes – a storming instrumental in the case of 'She's So Fine', a Hendrix-free mix for 'Little Miss Strange'. Rounding out the familiar material, the compilers reprised 'Red House' (Paris, 1968) from the long-lost *Stages* set, on the basis that it showcased Redding on guitar rather than bass.

The remaining songs were all previously unissued, at least officially. 'Dream' from December 1967 found Hendrix on bass and Redding imitating his leader's style on guitar. The same sessions produced 'There Ain't Nothing Wrong', featuring Dave Mason on sitar alongside the Experience, with a Redding vocal added in 1988 under Chas Chandler's supervision. Hendrix's guitar was the star attraction here, though, and the track was mixed accordingly.

During the *Electric Ladyland* sessions, Hendrix played bass and produced 'Walking Through The Garden', a whimsical piece of psychedelia featuring a thin Redding vocal. Jimi was entirely absent when Redding cut 'Little, Little Girl' in May 1968, but returned as producer for the quintessential UK psych offering 'How Can I Live?' that August. Rounding out a patchy but diverting album were two takes of 'Noel's Tune' from February 1969 – fiery hard rock, with some stirring Hendrix lead guitar on the first version, but Jimi back in the control room for the much less exciting second rendition.

Stephen Stills

Stephen Stills

LP release: Atlantic 2401 004 (UK), November 1970
CD release: Atlantic 7567-82809-2 (UK), October 1995

TRACK FEATURING HENDRIX: Old Times Good Times

HENDRIX AND BUFFALO SPRINGFIELD/CSNY MULTI-INSTRUMENTALIST Stephen Stills first met at the Monterey Pop Festival, and jammed several times over the next three years. Stills also took part in some Hendrix studio sessions, and can briefly be heard (for example) on 'My Friend' from *The Cry Of Love*. His regular sideman in recent decades, keyboardist Michael Finnigan, was also present at several Hendrix recording dates.

When Stills was assembling his first studio album in March 1970 at Olympic Studios in London, Hendrix was a natural choice for a cameo appearance. His contribution, 'Old Times Good Times', was actually overshadowed by the Stills/Clapton collaboration which followed it on the album, but since 1970 Stills has regularly claimed (a) that he has numerous other tracks from the same session, notably one called 'White Nigger', and (b) that he is about to release them. 'White Nigger' has subsequently circulated amongst CSNY fans, but only as a Hendrix-free re-recording from a later Stills solo project.

Index